THE MAGICAL WORLDS OF THE LORD OF THE RINGS

THE MAGICAL
WORLDS OF
THE LORD OF
THE RINGS

The Amazing Myths,
Legends, and Facts
Behind the Masterpiece

DAVID COLBERT

McArthur & Company
Toronto

Published in Canada by McArthur & Company,
322 King Street West, Suite 402,
Toronto, Ontario M5V 1J2.

National Library Cataloging-in-Publication Data

Colbert, David
The magical worlds of the Lord of the Rings : the amazing myths, legends, and facts behind the masterpiece / David Colbert.
ISBN 1-55278-340-5

1. Tolkien, J.R.R. (John Ronald Reuel), 1892–1973. Lord of the rings. I. Title.

PR6039.O32L63323 2002a   823'.912   C2002-903342-X

The Publisher would like to acknowledge the financial support of the Government of Canada through the Book Publishing Industry Development Program (BPIDP) and the Canada Council for our publishing activities.

for
BRENDA KNIGHT
Witch Bree
Galadriel
who thought of it

and for my editors
KIM WALTEMYER and AMANDA LI
who endured it

CONTENTS

INTRODUCTION

A FUNNY THING happened when the motion picture of *The Fellowship of the Ring* opened in December 2001. For years, while the three movies of *The Lord of the Rings* ("LOTR" from now on) were being made, Tolkien fans worried that the books would be ruined. To tell the story in just a few hours, they said, favorite characters and scenes would be cut. Big ideas would be ignored. Only people who had not read the books would like the films.

But when *Fellowship* opened, the loudest clapping in the theaters came from long-time fans. Along with the thrill ride of a great movie, they understood many of the tale's deeper meanings. Knowing the story by heart, they filled in the gaps with their imaginations.

Deeper meanings weren't obvious to the people who were new to Tolkien. Although they certainly liked the film, many wondered why devoted Tolkien fans make such a fuss about his brilliance. They didn't see any reason for the passionate debates that make Tolkien readers famous.

Their feelings are easy to understand. A computer graphic of a mountain can give a story a big setting, but it can't explain big ideas like immortality or fate. It can't reveal how Tolkien draws names from forgotten languages, or characters from ancient legends.

Even close readers of *LOTR* struggle with those questions, because all sorts of strange sources inspired Tolkien. For instance, a single word from Anglo-Saxon—a language that hasn't been used for centuries—inspired him to write a long story about the early years of Middle-earth. (The word and its meaning are explained on pages 138–139.) He also drew inspiration from legends told in faraway places, like the countryside of Finland. And he spent a lot of time making connections between the invented languages that are spoken in *LOTR*.

Tolkien had a big goal in mind when he looked into these ancient words and stories: he hoped to see the real events behind their first appearance. He thought that with enough digging, he might uncover an entire mythology—one to rival the mythologies of cultures such as ancient Greece and Rome.

That's a lot for a reader to absorb. Still, with the right guide you can easily understand the many remarkable details in *LOTR*. That's the point of this book. It's written both for people who know the story and for those who have only seen the films. It doesn't assume you start with much knowledge, yet it takes you deep into Tolkien's world to tell the stories behind the stories. Throughout, you'll find Tolkien's own thoughts. Some are revealed in letters to friends and editors. Many, however, were explanations offered directly to readers, who began to write to Tolkien with questions within a few weeks of the first publication of *The Hobbit* in 1937. At the time, no one could have foreseen Tolkien's amazing worldwide success. But even those early fans, casually picking up an unknown children's book, sensed that the story would be even more fascinating if they could find out something about the author and his ideas. You'll discover they were right.

Note: For those of you who haven't finished *LOTR*, or who are waiting for the final films, I've done my best to avoid "spoilers" (statements revealing big surprises in the plot). A spoiler about the end of *LOTR* appears at the end of this book. You've been warned! —D.C.

The Silmarillion, The Hobbit, and *The Lord of the Rings* are published in the U.S. by Houghton Mifflin. Page numbers for *LOTR* refer to the 1994 one-volume edition.

WHY DID TOLKIEN MAKE BILBO DISAPPEAR?

Baggins, Bilbo

AT THE START of *LOTR*, Bilbo Baggins puts on the Ring so he can disappear from his birthday party as if by magic. Soon after, it seems, he disappears from the story just as suddenly. We see him again only briefly, and when we do, we learn he has been spending his time reading old Elvish books and writing. If you haven't read *The Hobbit*, you might not realize he was quite an adventurer himself. The sword Sting, so deadly to Orcs, was his. He fought giant spiders, and a dragon. In fact, none of the events of *LOTR* could have happened without him: he was the one who found the Ring in Gollum's cave.

So why isn't he the hero of *LOTR*? How did our beloved Frodo come into the story?

WHAT'S SO FUNNY?

Actually, in Tolkien's first attempt at *LOTR*, Bilbo *was* the main character. The story was going to be another Bilbo adventure, to satisfy readers of *The Hobbit*. The idea was that Bilbo had spent all his fortune from the first adventure and needed to look for more.

Eventually Tolkien decided the story would be more serious. But that created a problem. It didn't fit with Bilbo, who is often a fun-loving prankster. For instance, his speech at his birthday party in *LOTR* is filled with jokes. Then he leaves behind gifts with notes that tease his family and friends.

Had it been Bilbo's task to return the Ring, readers would have expected the same comic adventure they had enjoyed in *The Hobbit*. They would have been disappointed. So to create a new mood, Tolkien shifted Bilbo aside.

EXIT BILBO, STAGE LEFT

That's when Tolkien introduced a new character, Bilbo's son. But that didn't work perfectly, either. Why would Bilbo let his son face danger? How would Tolkien explain where the son is during *The Hobbit*—or, more difficult, Bilbo's wife?

Tolkien says *LOTR* is a translation of an ancient book that started as Bilbo's private diaries. He called this book the *Red Book of Westmarch*—similar to an important ancient book in our world. The Welsh legends of King Arthur and others are found in the *Red Book of Hergest,* written in the 1300s.

Tolkien eventually found the answer in legends. Both history and literature have many examples of important uncles and nephews. This goes back to early times, when custom required that uncles play the role of guardian, in case a father died early (as often happened then). In legends, these nephews often become as great or greater than their uncles, and inspire stories of their own. King Arthur's nephew is Sir Gawain, the shining example of what Arthur desires in Knights of the Round Table: honor, wisdom, loyalty, and courtesy. The legends of Charlemagne, a medieval king of Europe, had tales about Charlemagne's nephew, Roland—another knight of tremendous bravery and loyalty. Charlemagne's niece,

Sir Gawain and the Green Knight is one of many Old English and Middle English poems Tolkien translated into modern English.

Bradamante, is also a great knight. The hero of *Beowulf*, an Old English poem that was an important source for *LOTR*, is the nephew of a king. He slays monsters no one else can defeat, and becomes king himself.

These favorite stories gave Tolkien the explanation he needed. Bilbo's replacement became a younger cousin, with the official status of nephew and heir.

It may have hurt Tolkien to retire Bilbo, but for the generation of fans who had already read *The Hobbit*, nothing less would have been convincing. It was time for a new hero. Enter Frodo.

See also:

Baggins, Frodo

Beowulf

Gollum

WHY IS FRODO THE RING-BEARER?

FROM THE FIRST moment we see Frodo and Aragorn together, at The Prancing Pony inn, we see how far Frodo falls short of being a classic hero. He is easily frightened by danger, while Aragorn is calm. He doesn't even seem clever enough to lead: unlike Aragorn, who has kept the secret identity of "Strider" for years, Frodo foolishly puts on the Ring and gives himself away just minutes after entering the inn as "Mr. Underhill."

That moment reveals a lot about both of them. Even by hobbit standards, Frodo doesn't stand out as special. He's not very strong or fast. He doesn't have the happy energy of Merry, Pippin, or Sam. He's shy. He seems bookish, like Bilbo.

Compare that to Aragorn. You can see at a

glance that Aragorn is a star. He's a natural leader. Battles have made him tough. He has the moral strength to resist the pull of the Ring.

Most important, Frodo doesn't want to be the Ring-bearer. He wishes the problem of the Ring would just go away. Aragorn, however, is itching to lead the fight. He faces Sauron in the palantír (seeing-stone), to defy him directly.

Though *LOTR* is often called a "trilogy," Tolkien never planned it as three books. His publisher decided it was too long to be printed as one.

Aragorn seems to be the perfect hero, and that's no accident. Tolkien deliberately gives him the qualities of many familiar heroes. Like King Arthur, or Moses, his royal birth is kept hidden from other characters until the time is right. The story of his broken sword is like the legend of a great hero of northern Europe, Sigurd. He can cure ills with a special

plant, as in the legends of King Charlemagne.

Yet, after going to all that trouble to make Aragorn more heroic than Frodo, Tolkien picked Frodo to carry the Ring. Why?

"Some Are Born Great . . ."

Tolkien broke the usual storytelling rules on purpose. He wanted his story to be about someone who becomes great because of qualities more important than size or strength. Although *LOTR* appears at first glance to be a great epic adventure, at its core is a fairy tale. "Nothing moves my heart," Tolkien wrote, "beyond all passions and heartbreaks of the world," as much as watching a character become noble—"from the Ugly Duckling to Frodo" (*The Letters of J.R.R. Tolkien* edited by H. Carpenter with C. Tolkien, 232). So he sends Frodo, a most unlikely hero, on a dangerous journey, a great quest, testing Frodo to the limit. Along the way, Frodo discovers noble qualities he never imagined he had: bravery, strength, determination, and patience.

This process of becoming noble fascinated Tolkien even more than the struggle of good against evil. He retells the Ugly Duckling fairy tale many times in *LOTR*, because he wants to see it happen again and again. That's why his focus switches from Frodo to Sam

In Tolkien's time, "baggings" was slang for "snacks"— something never far from the mind of a hobbit. That might be an origin for the last name "Baggins."

On the other hand, long before the hobbits were invented, Tolkien wrote a poem about a "Miss Biggins."

Gamgee towards the end of the story, and why Merry and Pippin also stop clowning around and acquire some noble qualities of their own.

Aragorn is born great; Frodo has greatness thrust upon him. That makes all the difference in the world to Tolkien. When the Fellowship is formed, Elrond Halfelven says, "This is the hour of the Shire-folk [hobbits], when they arise from their quiet fields to shake the towers and counsels of the great" (*The Lord of the Rings* by J.R.R. Tolkien, 264). In Tolkien's view, history is not always made by famous heroes and villains. Unknown individuals, like most of the hobbits, play crucial roles. And there is no role more crucial than bearing the One Ring.

See also:

Baggins, Bilbo

Names

Silmarillion, The

Swords

WHY IS FRODO IN CAVES SO OFTEN?

Baggins, Frodo

SPELUNKER. THAT'S THE kind of strange word Tolkien might have liked, and it describes many of his characters. A spelunker is a person who goes spelunking—or, more helpfully, someone who explores caves.

In *The Hobbit*, Bilbo Baggins explores many caves, from troll and goblin caves, to Gollum's cave, to an underground dungeon, and then a dragon's cave. In *LOTR*, Frodo is also a spelunker. On his journey, which is supposed to take him deep inside Mount Doom, he must pass safely through a barrow (a burial mound); the Dwarves' underground world; and mountain caves near Mordor. Sense a theme? Tolkien is

From their clothes to their horses and their language, Tolkien's Riders of the Mark are based on descriptions of Anglo-Saxons. Their emblem, a white horse on a green background, comes from a huge carving in a chalk hill not very far from Tolkien's home. More than 100 meters long, it was once thought to have been made by Saxons. (It is probably much older.) You can still see it today.

faithfully following a storytelling tradition. From the oldest legends to the most recent, heroes have stepped into frightening underworlds. An ancient Greek myth tells of Orpheus, who braves the three-headed guard dog of the underworld, Cerberus, to rescue his lover, Eurydice. In Homer's *Odyssey*, Odysseus's men enter a cave for safety, only to encounter the man-eating giant, Cyclops. In the Roman epic *Aeneid*, a hero who enters a cave to a fire-filled underworld is warned, "Summon up your courage, for you will need it." Since religion played a large part in

Tolkien's life, he even rewords for *LOTR* a few lines from a famous Bible story of an underground journey. In *LOTR*, Malbeth the Seer makes this prediction about a descent Aragorn will make:

> *The Tower trembles; to the tombs of kings*
> *doom approaches. The Dead awaken;*
> *for the hour is come for the oathbreakers:*
> *at the Stone of Erech they shall stand again*
> (*The Lord of the Rings* by J.R.R. Tolkien, 764).

In the Bible, after Jesus Christ is shut in a cave behind a great rock, the story reads almost the same:

> *The earth quaked, rocks were split,*
>   *tombs were opened,*
> *and the bodies of many saints who had*
>   *fallen asleep were raised.*
> *And coming forth from their tombs*
>   *after his resurrection, they entered*
>   *the holy city and appeared to many.*
> (Matthew 27:51–53)

When the Fellowship approaches the Golden Hall of the King of Rohan, Aragorn, often called a "wanderer" in *LOTR*, recites lines that echo an Anglo-Saxon poem called "The Wanderer." Tolkien was creating a history for that poem, as if it had been passed down since before the time of *LOTR*.

Other examples come right up to the present day. In one *Stars Wars* episode, Luke Skywalker enters a cave to find an imaginary Darth Vader. Harry Potter descends into the

In *Beowulf*, an important source for Tolkien, the title character goes underground (to the bottom of a lake, no less) to battle with a monster, then fights a cave-dwelling dragon.

Chamber of Secrets below the Hogwarts School and meets his enemy, Lord Voldemort.

Scholar Joseph Campbell, who studied legends all over the world to find similarities, says underground journeys are a trademark of heroes. As he describes it, to step into a cave is to dare to look at the dark parts of one's own mind and soul. The darkness hides what is unknown—not only within the cave, but within one's self. Sometimes the dangers are the hero's worst nightmares brought to life. Other times, those dangers are too awful to have been imagined. Aragorn, who is frightened by very little, remains haunted by his first journey into Moria. When Gandalf is dragged into an abyss by the Balrog, he discovers that "Far, far below the deepest delvings of the Dwarves, the world is gnawed by nameless things. Even Sauron knows them not" (*The Lord of the Rings* by J.R.R. Tolkien, 490).

See also:

Beowulf

Orcs

In all these cases, from both legend and *LOTR*, Campbell's insight proves true: the heroes face more than just monsters when they step underground. The greater battle is against their own doubts and fears.

WHICH
EPIC POEM
INSPIRED
TOLKIEN?

Beowulf

YOU MIGHT NEVER have read *LOTR* if not for a thousand-year-old poem that deeply influenced all of Tolkien's work.

The poem is entitled *Beowulf*. It is one of few surviving examples of Old English, also known as Anglo-Saxon, a language brought to Britain in about A.D. 449 by invading tribes from Europe. ("Anglo-Saxon" comes from the names of the tribes: Angles, Saxons, and Jutes.) Though it was common in Britain for more than six hundred years, it is very different from the English we speak today. Outside of universities, no one takes the trouble to learn it. Tolkien, however, happened to be one of the world's experts. He taught it at Oxford University for many years.

Beowulf makes up almost one-tenth of all the Anglo-Saxon poetry that survives today.

A STORY OF MERRIE OLD . . . DENMARK?

If you haven't read *Beowulf* yet, here's a bit of background, starting with an odd fact. This poem that is so important to English literature is set entirely outside England. All the action takes place in Scandinavia, because the poem is based on legends brought to England along with the new language.

Set in an age of war between the Danes, Swedes, and a tribe called the Geats (from what is now southern Sweden), much of the poem is devoted to fights between the Geat warrior Beowulf and three creatures. The main events run as follows:

—A huge mead hall, where Danish warriors meet to drink and feast, is terrorized by a monster named Grendel. The Geat warrior Beowulf offers to fight the monster, and mortally wounds it before it runs off.

—The next day, while the warriors celebrate, the monster's mother comes for revenge. Beowulf fights the mother, pursues her to the bottom of a foul pond, kills her, and then returns with both her head and the head of Grendel, who has died.

—Many years later, when Beowulf is king, a fire-breathing dragon begins to destroy his realm. The dragon wants revenge because someone has stolen a golden cup from his pile

Considered the oldest work of literature in English, *Beowulf* was probably composed in the eighth century. Just one copy of the Old English text, set down about two hundred years later, survives today. It is in the British Museum.

of treasure. Beowulf slays the dragon, but dies from a wound he receives in the fight.

The poem is much more than just a string of fight scenes, of course. It remains the most famous work of its time because of its style, its revealing details, and its grand themes. Tolkien has borrowed bits of all of these.

BEOWULF IN TOLKIEN

The Hobbit began as little more than a bedtime story for his children, so Tolkien was relaxed about how he used bits of *Beowulf* at first. If anything, you could say he was having fun with it, turning it into something much less serious than the original. (No sense in causing bad dreams.) Still, as he told editors of the *Observer* after *The Hobbit* was published, "*Beowulf* is among my most valued sources" (*The Letters of J.R.R. Tolkien* edited by H. Carpenter with C. Tolkien, 31). For *LOTR*, he gave more thought to *Beowulf*'s meaning, and kept its serious mood. You can see the poem's influence in both books:

There are similar settings. In *The Hobbit*, a crucial confrontation takes place in a dragon's lair. Both *The Hobbit* and *LOTR* prominently feature mead halls, where warriors drink and feast. As Tolkien expert Thomas Shippey notes, in *LOTR* the Elf Legolas describes Meduseld

Before Old English arrived with the Anglo-Saxons in the mid-400s A.D., most Britons spoke forms of Celtic.

Old English changed into Middle English as new words arrived with the Norman (French) Conquest of 1066. Modern English began to appear in about the mid-1400s.

Beowulf is also responsible for Tolkien being "discovered." One of his former students, hired to translate the poem, casually mentioned to her publisher that Tolkien had written a children's book similar to it. *The Hobbit* was at the printers not long afterwards.

(the Golden Hall) with the same line that describes the mead hall in *Beowulf*: "The light of it shines far over the land" (*The Lord of the Rings* by J.R.R. Tolkien, 496).

Characters and names are drawn from the poem. Frodo's name appears in *Beowulf.* Beorn, a human chief in *The Hobbit,* is like Beowulf himself, at his most ferocious. The name of Tolkien's Orcs come from *orcneas,* a word used for monsters in *Beowulf.*

Plot points are also duplicated. When Bilbo Baggins is in the dragon's lair in *The Hobbit,* he steals a cup, just as a cup was stolen from the dragon in *Beowulf.* The dragon's response in *Beowulf*—to emerge from his cave and lay

The monster Grendel— a terror to Danes, Swedes, and Geats alike.

waste to the countryside—is repeated in *The Hobbit.* A similar thing happens in the sec- ond-to-last chapter of *LOTR.* (For the sake of those who haven't finished reading, the details won't be mentioned here.)

When in *LOTR* a sword plunged into a Black Rider seems to be dissolved by the wickedness within him, we're seeing exactly what happens to Beowulf's sword when it touches the blood of the horrible monster Grendel. And Tolkien gives the idea a neat twist when a Black Rider makes his own sword melt after it pierces Frodo's shoulder.

Also, as Shippey notes, the rules that the Fellowship must follow when approaching the King of the Golden Hall—checking in with certain guards, leaving weapons behind—are the same "down to minute detail" as in *Beowulf* (*The Road to Middle-earth* by T. A. Shippey, 95).

Themes from Beowulf *appear in Tolkien's work.* In *LOTR,* as in *Beowulf,* feuding tribes set aside their differences to fight common enemies. And in both stories, the heroes must resist turning into the monsters they fight.

For some readers, *Beowulf* is a chore, an old book to read for school. That's too bad. For

Tolkien, it was anything but work. Year after year, he read it to new students. And when he did, the effect was magical. "He could turn a lecture room into a mead hall in which he was the bard and we were the feasting, listening guests," said one former student (*Tolkien* by H. Carpenter, 133). Another, the poet W. H. Auden, later thanked his teacher: "I don't think I have ever told you what an unforgettable experience it was for me as an undergraduate, hearing you recite *Beowulf*. The voice was the voice of Gandalf" (*Tolkien* by H. Carpenter, 133).

That's the sign of a great teacher: with what inspired him, he inspired others. And now that you've read *LOTR*, you too have feasted in the mead hall.

See also:

Names

Swords

WHY DO DWARVES AND ELVES DISLIKE EACH OTHER?

Dwarves

AT THE START of *LOTR*, Gimli the Dwarf and Legolas the Elf are suspicious of each other. Their races have been feuding for most of the history of Middle-earth—so long that no one seems to remember how the trouble began.

SHADOWS AND LIGHT

The ancient feud actually goes back to old legends in our world about dwarves and elves, which Tolkien gave an original twist. In those legends, as in *LOTR*, dwarves are miners and smiths—dwellers in the underground world of rock and ore. They are tough, and usually short. As one writer describes:

> Ugly, long-nosed, and of a dirty brown color . . . their language was the echo of solitudes, and their dwelling-places subterranean caves and clefts. They were particularly distinguished for a knowledge of the mysterious powers of nature, and for the runes which they carved and explained. They were the most skilful artificers of all created beings, and worked in metals and in wood.

You can easily recognize the Dwarves of Middle-earth in that description: they live underground, they speak their own difficult language and use runes as an alphabet, and they are skilled craftsmen.

Legendary dwarves are also combative like those of Middle-earth. They are possessive of the gold they mine. They don't trust others easily. As one folklore expert writes, "[T]he dwarfs do at times have dealings with mankind, yet on the whole they seem to shrink from man; they give the impression of a downtrodden afflicted race, which is on the point of abandoning its ancient home to new and more powerful invaders."

It took Tolkien twelve years to write *The Lord of the Rings*. Four more passed before the first volume finally appeared in 1954.

Jealousy is behind many of the fights between dwarves and elves in Norse legends. As one author puts it, Norse elves "loved the light, were kindly disposed to mankind, and generally appeared as fair and lovely children." But the dwarves "appeared only at night. They avoided the sun as a deadly enemy, because whenever his beams fell upon any of them they changed immediately into stones." Dwarves envy elves; but they also look down on what seems to them an easy life.

There also seems to be a bit of jealousy behind the feud in *LOTR*. In the legend Tolkien invented to explain the origin of his Dwarves, they are not the favorites of Ilúvatar, the God of Middle-earth. Elves are. Dwarves are actually made by one of the Valar, the angelic spirits who shape Middle-earth. He is impatient to have creatures to teach, so he tries to take on the role of God and create some. This angers Ilúvatar, who was planning to make Elves. And though Ilúvatar allows the Dwarves to live, he says they must sleep in the earth until the Elves are alive, and that "often strife shall arise between thine [Dwarves] and mine [Elves]" (*The Silmarillion* by J.R.R. Tolkien, 44).

But legends are only a starting point for Tolkien in this case. The story of *LOTR* settles

Tolkien liked to capitalize his versions of Dwarves and Elves, to emphasize that they aren't exactly like the ones in legend.

the fight. The Fellowship of the Ring is formed when Elves and Dwarves are faced with an evil so great that their feud is unimportant. They know, as the Elf Haldir says, "in nothing is the power of the Dark Lord more clearly shown than in the estrangement that divides all those who still oppose him" (*The Lord of the Rings* by J.R.R. Tolkien, 339). And once forced together, Gimli and Legolas become great friends. That was Tolkien's design as a writer. He would say it is also part of Ilúvatar's plan.

See also:
Elves
Galadriel
Names

WHY ARE TOLKIEN'S ELVES TALL?

IF YOUR FIRST experience of Tolkien was a *LOTR* film, you might have wondered why the Elves are so tall. They're even taller than humans. But shouldn't they be smaller than hobbits? We think of elves as little folk, like fairies: small creatures who live in a magical world. They aren't like the creatures of *LOTR*: great in size and wisdom, admired by nearly every other race. So why would Tolkien call his characters "Elves"?

As it happens, Tolkien was following a tradition from long ago. Before elves and fairies became the little creatures we know from storybooks, they were thought to be a lot like the Elves of Middle-earth.

In real life, the actor who plays Gimli the Dwarf in the *LOTR* films (John Rhys-Davies) is taller than the actor who plays Legolas the Elf (Orlando Bloom).

29

"MORE BRILLIANT THAN THE SUN"

Tolkien's Elves follow the tradition of Norse legends. As one writer says, Norse elves are "inferior to the gods, but still possessed of great power." Some are "exceedingly fair, more brilliant than the sun."

Celtic mythology, which may have been based on those Norse legends, also influenced Tolkien. His Elves are similar to the Tuatha Dé Danaan (People of the Goddess Danu), said to have arrived in Ireland before humans. The descendants of the Tuatha Dé Danaan, known as the Sidhe, are also like Tolkien's noble creatures. Both of these Celtic races, like the Norse elves, play a role that appears in many religions: they are more gifted than humans, but not quite gods. However, they fell out of favor as a new religion arrived.

HONEY, I SHRUNK THE ELVES!

As Europe became primarily Christian, people stopped believing that any creatures stood between humans and God. Stories of great elves and fairies were pushed aside. In Geoffrey Chaucer's *The Canterbury Tales*, written in the 1300s, a character says, with regret:

In the old days of King Arthur
Of which Britons speak with honor

LOTR is about a half million words long. Tolkien read a lot of it aloud to friends while he was working on it. (It would probably take you more than two days and nights of continuous reading to do it all at once.)

All this land was filled with fairies.
The elf-queen, with her jolly company,
Danced often in many a green meadow. . . .
I speak of many hundreds of years ago.
Now because of the great charity and
  prayers
Of the holy friars, there are no elves
  to be seen.

However, the idea of magical creatures didn't disappear completely. In time, elves and fairies came to be associated with smaller concerns—matters that were puzzling, but not nearly important enough for God. They became house spirits: creatures to blame if a plate was mysteriously broken, or to be thanked for a run of good luck.

That's how elves were being described in the late 1500s, when the work of a particular writer made sure those folk tales would last.

THE HOBGOBLINS OF LITTLE MINDS

Tolkien forever blamed William Shakespeare for making silly elves and fairies a part of literature. To be fair, Shakespeare was not the first person to write about tiny fairies. But Shakespeare did it often, and he did it so well that the idea stuck. The best example is his play *A Midsummer Night's Dream*, set in an

Edmund Spenser's *The Faerie Queen,* one of the last great works about majestic elves and fairies, appeared about the time of Shakespeare's plays. In this tale, the Greek god Prometheus creates the first "Elfe," who then meets a great Fairy. From them, *"a mighty people soon grew, and powerful kings"* (Book II, canto 9).

enchanted forest. The friendly hobgoblin Puck describes tiny elves that are easily frightened, and "creep into acorn-cups and hide." Small fairies also appear in many other Shakespeare plays. Tolkien, who loved the idea of magnificent Elves, hated Shakespeare's elves and fairies. He told one reader that what Shakespeare did was "unforgivable" (*The Letters of J.R.R. Tolkien* edited by H. Carpenter with C. Tolkien, 185).

THE AIR UP THERE

Tolkien worried that he could not change our ideas about tiny elves. Still, he tried. He gave his creatures many special qualities. They are like highly refined humans. They are intelligent and sensitive, and over the years have gradually acquired great knowledge. Just as in the old legends, they are superior to humans. And though both races look the same when they are first created, over time the Elves come to be shaped by their "greater wisdom, and skill, and beauty" (*The Silmarillion* by J.R.R. Tolkien, 121). That's how they grew so tall.

See also:

Dwarves

Galadriel

Rings

WHY DO ELVES LIVE SO LONG?

Elves

MANY CHARACTERS IN *LOTR* have long lives. Aragorn has already lived more than one human lifetime when the story opens. Hobbits usually live twice as long as humans. When *LOTR* begins, Bilbo is getting old even for a hobbit—though he seems younger because of the Ring's power. Gollum is about 500 years old, also thanks to the Ring.

The Elves are even older. They may look young, but some are many thousands of years old. In fact, they are immortal. If they are killed, their spirits come back in bodies just like the ones they had before, and they even have the same memories. Tolkien made very careful rules about the immortality of the Elves, because the subject was important to him. But his opinions about it might seem unexpected.

Tolkien said he wished he could have written *LOTR* entirely in Elvish. He didn't create that many words, but he did invent enough to let you have a simple conversation in it. Some people go so far as to write poetry in Elvish.

FOREVER AND EVER, AMEN

As Tolkien explained it, Ilúvatar wanted to see how different races would feel about life and death—especially Elves and humans. Oddly enough, both races envy each other. The humans, of course, envy the immortality of the Elves. Meanwhile, the Elves find that living forever can get boring. Also, they have to

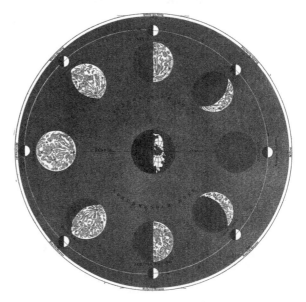

watch all the things they love pass away. And it is painful to witness so many centuries of evil. As Tolkien puts it, the Elves envy the "escape" offered humans from "the weariness of Time" (*The Letters of J.R.R. Tolkien* edited by H. Carpenter with C. Tolkien, 205).

DEATH, BE NOT PROUD

You may wonder why this subject obsessed Tolkien. The answer may be that humans have always created stories to explain away the mystery of death. Or maybe Tolkien became fascinated about it through his religion. Certain ideas about death in *LOTR* show a Catholic point of view. For instance, the Valar have promised that humankind and Elves will have some part in Ilúvatar's next creation; so to fear death is to lose faith in God. According to Tolkien, that's just as bad in our world as it is in Middle-earth.

By the time World War I ended in 1918, all of Tolkien's close friends but one had been killed. Tolkien was just twenty-six years old at the time.

But perhaps there's a more personal reason. Tolkien was an orphan. His father died when Tolkien was only four years old. His mother died when Tolkien was twelve. Naturally, these events left deep and permanent wounds. They may explain why Tolkien thought so much about the issues of life and death. They could also explain the beliefs he

See also:

Undying Lands

presents in *LOTR* though his Elves—that death is nothing to fear, and living forever is not necessarily a thing to be envied. In fact, humans are blessed to have lives that come to a natural end.

WHAT MAKES A FOREST WALK?

Ents

IT'S A GOOD bet that Tolkien's favorite color was green, given the many examples of trees and forests in *LOTR*. He even included trees with minds, like Old Man Willow, and the tree-like giants, the Ents. Tolkien's love of trees began at an early age. As a child, he imagined them as characters in stories, and loved tales in which trees played important roles. One that interested him a lot was William Shakespeare's play *Macbeth*, about an ambitious lord in Scotland who commits murder to become king. In the play, Macbeth is visited by a ghost who tells the future. The ghost says Macbeth will not be defeated unless a particular forest travels to fight him. This delights Macbeth. He reassures himself

William
Shakespeare
(1564–1616)

that a forest could never actually move:

> *Macbeth:* That will never be.
> Who can impress the forest, bid the tree
> Unfix his earth-bound root?

Macbeth shouldn't be so relaxed. Near the end of the play, a watchman runs to Macbeth, frightened and confused by what he has seen: a moving forest is heading towards Macbeth's castle. Soon Macbeth learns the forest is not

made of living trees, but rather a rival army, disguised with branches and leaves from the trees of the forest that the ghost named. Just as the ghost predicted, the army defeats Macbeth.

Shakespeare's story fascinated Tolkien, but it also disappointed him. He wanted a *real* forest to fight Macbeth. "I longed to devise a setting in which trees might really march to war," he explained (*The Letters of J.R.R. Tolkien* edited by H. Carpenter with C. Tolkien, 212). That's just what he did.

So, what makes a forest walk? In Tolkien, as in Shakespeare, forests walk when they become angry at an evil ruler.

"THE OLD WORKS OF GIANTS"

Even more interesting than the walking trees are the tree-herds who keep watch over them. The Ents, who look a lot like trees themselves, are giants. Treebeard is fourteen feet tall. That makes sense: their name comes from the Old English word for "giant"— *enta*. The word appears in a phrase used often by Anglo-Saxon poets, *eald enta geweorc*, meaning "the old works of giants." It refers to mysterious monuments or buildings left behind by ancient, unknown civilizations. For instance, you might say the circle of stone slabs at Stonehenge is an "old work of giants."

Just as the Anglo-Saxons didn't know the origin of those works, Ents are a mystery to the other creatures of Middle-earth. Tolkien never fully explains their creation in *LOTR*. After the story was published, he told readers that Ents are the oldest creatures of Middle-earth, made by the angelic spirits at the same time as the Eagles. But within the story itself, he wanted to leave the mystery unexplained,

Treebeard's blustery speaking style is meant as a private joke, according to biographer Humphrey Carpenter. It mimics the voice of Tolkien's friend C. S. Lewis, author of *The Lion, the Witch and the Wardrobe.*

just like "the old works of giants." That's part
of the charm of the Ents.

TOWN AND COUNTRY

Angry forests, protective Ents: Tolkien's devotion to nature could be fierce. He hated the
harm done to the countryside by the Indus-
trial Revolution—the movement to build
large factories, which began in the century of
his birth. "There's some devilry at work in the
Shire," says Sam, when factories appear as an
image in the Mirror of Galadriel (*The Lord of
the Rings* by J.R.R. Tolkien, 353). There may
have been a very personal reason for Tolkien's
passion.

When he was eight years old, around the

time he was imagining stories in which trees could speak, his family moved to the countryside outside Birmingham. For four years, Tolkien and his brother delighted in the greenery around their cottage. That time, Tolkien said, was "the longest-seeming and most formative part of my life" (*Tolkien* by H. Carpenter, 24).

Unfortunately, that era ended abruptly and in the worst possible way. Tolkien's mother died. Tolkien and his brother were then sent to Birmingham to live with an aunt. From the window in his new home, Tolkien saw factory smokestacks instead of trees. As biographer Humphrey Carpenter says, Tolkien's "love for the memory of the countryside of his youth" became "intimately bound up with his love for the memory of his mother" (*Tolkien* by H. Carpenter, 33). Knowing this, it's easy to understand Tolkien's desire to make the world green again.

See also:

Elves

WHAT DID TOLKIEN SEE IN GALADRIEL?

THOUGH GIMLI IS usually a rock-hard Dwarf, he shows a soft side when it comes to Galadriel. He can't help but admire her. You might even say he adores her, the way one adores a mother. That's appropriate. Galadriel is connected to several mother characters in legend and history.

MAN VERSUS NATURE

Galadriel's primary role in Middle-earth is to create and sustain the Elves' home, Lothlórien. This makes her what historians call an Earth Mother. From the very earliest myths, Earth Mother goddesses have been credited with creating and nourishing life. The Egyptians worshipped Isis; the Assyrians revered Ishtar; the Greeks were sustained by Gaea,

Isis, Egyptian mother god.

Hera, and Demeter; the Romans honored Maia, Ceres and others. This Earth Mother idea appears in legends from all over the world. Few cultures give male gods the same role—just as Galadriel's husband, Celeborn, doesn't sustain Lothlórien.

O MOTHER, WHERE ART THOU?

Tolkien carefully chose the date that the Fellowship begins its mission to overthrow Sauron: December 25, the same day Christians celebrate the Virgin Mary giving birth to Jesus.

Tolkien, a devout Catholic, also gave Galadriel qualities of a particular mother who was important to him: the Blessed Virgin Mary, mother of Jesus Christ. Mary symbolized for Tolkien the same things that Galadriel offers Frodo and his companions: divine compassion and wisdom. She returns

their devotion with her own. "[T]he Lady Galadriel is above all the jewels that lie beneath the earth," says Gimli, who has been moved to tears by her decency (*The Lord of the Rings* by J.R.R. Tolkien, 347).

Galadriel wasn't the first Mary figure Tolkien created for his Middle-earth. In his original legends (later collected into *The Silmarillion*), that role belonged to Varda, one of the most powerful of the Valar, the angelic spirits who shape Middle-earth. (Varda is the character who is being called for help when the characters say *"A Elbereth Gilthoniel!"*) In fact, Elves revere Varda the way Galadriel is revered by Gimli and Frodo. But Tolkien wanted all the Valar to stay out of the action of *LOTR* as much as possible—even Varda. So Galadriel's part grew until she took on the Mary role. It's interesting that even with Varda out of the story Tolkien's instincts led him to give the Fellowship a mother figure.

In the *LOTR* films, Arwen speaks Elvish as Tolkien meant it to be spoken. All the actors learned real Elvish words, and spoke them using Tolkien's pronunciation.

MARY, MARY, QUITE CONTRARY

The Virgin Mary was an important influence on Tolkien's creation of Galadriel, but only one. The story of a different Bible character named Mary reveals another essential detail of Galadriel's character.

Galadriel regrets having rebelled against

the Valar as a youth, and her feelings are important to the story: if she still felt rebellious, she might want to keep the Ring when Frodo offers it to her, because it would make her very powerful. (In fact, she knows that she risks a lot by refusing it. If Frodo destroys it, her own Ring will lose its power, and her safe haven for the Elves will disappear. If he doesn't, Sauron might win it back, which would be worse. Either way, her refusal of the Ring is a sacrifice.) Tolkien called her a "penitent"—a term in Catholicism for those who regret their sins (*The Letters of J.R.R. Tolkien* edited by H. Carpenter with C. Tolkien, 407). She is like a famous penitent in the Bible, Mary Magdalene, a sinner who came to accept Christ and accompanied him in his final days. And like Mary Magdalene, Galadriel is forgiven by the Valar when they see she refuses Frodo's offer.

See also:

Religion

Silmarillion, The

WHY CAN'T YOU TRUST GALADRIEL'S MIRROR?

"GO NOT TO the Elves for counsel, for they will say both no and yes," says Frodo, repeating a hobbit proverb (*The Lord of the Rings* by J.R.R. Tolkien, 83). The Mirror of Galadriel is a perfect example: it offers only a hint of what path you should take. The visions in it are confusing. Are you looking at the past, the present, or the future? What *will* happen, or what *might* happen? That trickiness comes right out of legend, as do other qualities Tolkien gave the mirror.

WHO'S THE LOVELIEST OF ALL?

Mirrors have been connected with magic for thousands of years. Though it's hard to imagine now, they were once very rare and expensive. Most people went their whole life

without looking in a proper one. A very good reflection could even be frightening: sometimes people believed the mirror had captured their souls. But the same notion of magical power attracted wizards, who stared into mirrors until their sight became fuzzy, hoping visions of the future might appear.

This mix of history and superstition led to some of the great mirrors you know from literature, such as the evil queen's mirror in *Snow White*. The wizard Merlin of the King Arthur tales also has a magic mirror. Recently, the magical Mirror of Erised plays an important part in J. K. Rowling's *Harry Potter and the Sorcerer's Stone*.

The practice of staring into a mirror to see the future is called "scrying."

MOTHER KNOWS BEST

The Mirror of Galadriel is what's called an oracle—a person or object able to show the future. From ancient epics like Homer's *Odyssey* to recent films such as *The Matrix*, heroes have stopped along their journeys to consult an oracle. This was once also true in real life. Before waging war or making a long journey, people commonly asked oracles what might happen. In the ancient world, you could find them all over the place—there were more than 250 in Greece alone.

The most famous one in history was at

Delphi, in Greece. Supposedly, vapors rising from the ground had the power to put people in touch with certain gods. A temple was built on that spot, so a priestess could breathe the same vapors and contact the gods whenever someone wanted to ask a question. The Delphic oracle was taken very seriously. People sought advice there for twelve centuries.

It makes sense that Galadriel is the character who can show a glimpse of the future. In legend and in history—Delphi is a good example—the gift of prophecy is commonly connected to women. This derived from the ancient belief that women, being able to bear

The Delphic oracle was said to make contact with several gods, including an ancient, unnamed earth mother; the goddess Gaea, a later earth mother; Apollo; and Dionysus.

One expert says, "For several generations the Delphic oracle was the greatest spiritual power in Greece."

children, were closer to the forces of nature that ultimately control the world. In Roman legend, priestesses known as Sibyls were as respected as the Delphic oracle. The books containing their predictions were the most valuable volumes in the empire.

Until recently, modern scientists believed the idea of the Delphic oracle was foolish. But they have discovered that a sweet-smelling gas was indeed released from the ground under the temple. That gas, ethylene, can cause a trance, just as the ancient scholars described.

WANT A SECOND OPINION?

Galadriel warns that her mirror isn't trustworthy. That was a common fault of oracles in real life, often because the advice was worded in a way that could be easily misunderstood. For example, kings in the ancient world sometimes started wars after being told they would win great fame; but in the end, their fame came from being defeated. The same thing happens in literature. If you're a *Harry Potter* fan, you know the Mirror of Erised shows you not what *will* happen, but what you *want* to happen. ("Erised" is the mirror image of "Desire.")

"[A]dvice is a dangerous gift, even from the wise to the wise," says Gildor the Elf to Frodo (*The Lord of the Rings* by J.R.R. Tolkien, 83). No matter how much humankind wants to know what's coming, there is always a complication. Galadriel was right to warn Frodo against acting upon what he had seen.

WHO (OR WHAT) IS GANDALF?

Gandalf

READERS LOVE GANDALF, and it's easy to see why: he's wise, he's kind, he's strong, and, not least, he's very funny. People don't just admire him; they want to *be* him. At any large gathering of *LOTR* fans, you're likely to see a few dressed in Gandalf costumes: cloaks, peaked caps, fake beards, and long walking sticks.

Yet, for all the attention he gets, he's still a mystery. And he seems to like it that way. "I am not going to give an account of all my doings to you," he tells Frodo when they first talk about the Ring (*The Lord of the Rings* by J.R.R. Tolkien, 55). Everyone thinks he is just a wizard or a special Elf, though neither guess is right. As it happens, he is not only a mystery in Middle-earth. Tolkien's ideas about him are also difficult to see at first.

As part of the Hugo Awards (the most prestigious in science-fiction writing), the Gandalf Award is given for lifetime achievement. The first author to receive the honor was Tolkien.

A SORCERER'S APPRENTICE?

From appearances alone, many readers assume Tolkien based Gandalf on the sorcerer Merlin in the tales of King Arthur. Both characters look like classic wizards: old men with flowing robes and wild beards. Both like nature. They teach young heroes. Finally, we know that Tolkien had a great fondness for Welsh, the original language of the Merlin tales.

But the similarities aren't the whole story. For example, Merlin uses magic in the same way as, say, Harry Potter's teacher Albus Dumbledore. Using spells and incantations, he can heal wounds or control other people. Gandalf has supernatural gifts, but not because he has mastered sorcery. It only appears that way to hobbits. His powers come

With a walking stick like Gandalf's and Odin's, Merlin protects King Arthur from a faceless enemy.

from a higher source than Merlin's or Dumbledore's. As Aragorn tells Frodo, "Gandalf is greater than you Shire-folk know—as a rule you can only see his jokes and toys" (*The Lord of the Rings* by J.R.R. Tolkien, 169).

A NORSE ORIGIN?

To understand Gandalf, you need to look to the gods. A starting point is Norse mythology's most powerful god, Odin.

There are many connections between Odin and Gandalf. Odin is also depicted as a long-bearded old man, often with a walking stick. He has supernatural power. Not only is he able to read the carved alphabet of runes like Gandalf, he is the one who gave the gift of runes to humankind. Like Gandalf, he seems to be wandering alone on a quest that others cannot understand.

However, there are important differences:

—Odin is the supreme god in Scandinavian legend. Gandalf, on the other hand, seems to be following orders from a higher authority.

—Odin is often cruel, even barbaric. Human sacrifices are made to him. Gandalf always shows compassion and mercy.

—Odin loves treasure. Gandalf has no interest in wealth.

While on a hiking trip in Switzerland, Tolkien found a postcard showing a white-bearded mountain man, wearing a cloak and a wide-brimmed hat. That image sparked the creation of Gandalf.

—Odin possesses talents Gandalf doesn't share, such as the power to turn himself into a snake, an eagle, and other creatures.

As Tolkien himself once put it, Gandalf is "Odinic," meaning he is similar to Odin, though not quite the same (*The Letters of J.R.R. Tolkien* edited by H. Carpenter with C. Tolkien, 119). The differences between the two are as important as the similarities. Once again, Gandalf proves elusive. However, the fact that he's so slippery is the clue to his real origin.

A SECRET MISSION

Gandalf never reveals his true role in the plan to destroy the One Ring because he's not allowed. The Valar have ordered him to be

Just as Gandalf's horse Shadowfax was the fastest horse on Earth, Odin rode the fastest horse in Norse mythology, the eight-legged Sleipnir.

mysterious. He obeys them because he's actually working for them.

As Tolkien explained in letters to readers, Gandalf is actually an angel, sent to Middle-earth on a mission. The Valar want to help the creatures of Middle-earth resist Sauron, so they send spirits to Middle-earth to do some gentle prodding. Gandalf and some other angels, together called Istari, share that task. (Saruman was one of them, before he became Sauron's servant.) But the Valar don't want to push anyone around, or frighten them the way Sauron does. The Istari are told to keep their true identities a secret. This rule means the creatures of Middle-earth must decide to fight Sauron because it is the right thing to do, not because they fear the Valar.

Being an angel doesn't make Gandalf perfect, or give him knowledge of how the story will end. As he says often, there is a lot he does not know, even about his own task. For all his gifts, he can only hope for the best. And he, like the other members of the Fellowship, is being tested. He passes that test when he sacrifices himself by battling the fiery Balrog so his friends can escape. He actually dies, because the bodies the Istari are given to hide their identities make them as vulnerable as other creatures; but because of his generous

Gandalf dresses differently when he rejoins his friends, because he has risen a grade in the Istari. He is Gandalf the White, one step up from Gandalf the Grey. (Now you know why those Gandalf fans aren't all dressed alike.)

See also:

Names

Silmarillion

act, his spirit is placed in a new body and he is given even greater powers than before. Gandalf's friends notice small changes in his appearance because he is truly a new being.

HOW DID TOLKIEN THINK UP GOLLUM?

Gollum

WHEN GOLLUM IS on the scene, he's the focus of our attention. As sickening as an Orc and much more annoying, he has slick skin and webbed feet that bring to mind a large toad. Sometimes it's hard to remember he was once an ordinary hobbit. Yet, for all our disgust, we can't help pitying him, because we know he is a victim of the Ring. And his dangerous split personality is fascinating. Which side of it will triumph? Will Gollum help Frodo and Sam, or harm them?

Gollum's original hobbit name, Sméagol, is Old English for "burrower" or "digger"— a fitting name for a creature that takes to an extreme the hobbit habit of living in a hole.

SLIPPERY WHEN WET

Norse mythology was the first inspiration for many of the facts about Gollum's life and personality. You may recall that his past is as ugly as he is: corrupted almost as soon as he sees the Ring, he lives with the Ring for almost five hundred years—a lot of that time in a wet cave—before it is taken from him by Bilbo, leaving him upset and eager to get it back. Norse legends tell of another small, greedy, cave-dwelling character with a special ring and a desire for revenge. He appears in a story that was one of Tolkien's favorites as a child, "The Story of Sigurd" from Andrew Lang's *The Red Fairy Book*. The story goes as follows:

Andvari was King of the Dwarves, guardian of a magical ring and the treasure that the ring produced. He kept the treasure in an underground cave. The god Loki, asked to steal the treasure, ventured into the cave and caught Andvari. The dwarf gave up all the treasure except the magic ring, knowing the ring would replace what had been lost. But Loki demanded the ring too.

Andvari was furious. He cursed the treasure and the ring so that it would bring misfortune and death to anyone who kept it.

Loki warned the king for whom he had stolen the treasure of Andvari's curse: even "heroes unborn"—meaning future generations—would be doomed. But the king was

Sméagol's best friend's name is Déagol, the Old English word for "secret." That makes sense. His murder is Gollum's secret.

not frightened: "This glittering gold I shall keep as long as I live, and without fear of your threats. Go away!"

The king should have been less sure of himself. The threats proved true. As Andrew Lang tells the story, even the hero Sigurd— "whom no ten men could have slain in fair fight"—could not put a stop to the curse of this "fatal golden ring."

Doesn't the dwarf king Andvari sound a lot like Gollum? And here's a final clue. Tolkien reminds us again and again in *LOTR* that Gollum is hungry for "fishes." In the legend of Andvari, the dwarf didn't just live in

See also:

Rings

any cave; he lived in one with a waterfall and a pond full of fish. He often used magic to take the form of a large fish himself, so he could catch the smaller ones to eat.

WAS GOLLUM EVER GOOD?

THINK YOU'VE MET Gollum? Think again. The character that you know is not the character first introduced in *The Hobbit*. In fact, the first Gollum was so different you might even say he was good—or at least a little better.

THE LOST GOLLUM

The changes started to happen soon after *The Hobbit* was first published, when Tolkien began work on *LOTR*. His idea for *LOTR* was to have Bilbo return the ring that he found in Gollum's cave during the first adventure.

This got Tolkien thinking about the ring. He began to see it as the powerful, dark force we know from *LOTR*. But there was a problem. In the original version of *The Hobbit*, Gollum lets Bilbo have the ring too easily,

More than a decade before writing *The Hobbit*, Tolkien wrote a poem that includes a creature called Glip, who looks a lot like Gollum.

offering it as a prize in a contest of wits. That doesn't fit with *LOTR*. The One Ring is supposed to be irresistible. No one would give it up so quickly, especially not Gollum.

Tolkien noticed the problem soon after starting to write *LOTR*, but he decided to press on anyway. He worked on *LOTR* for ten years while the public enjoyed the original version of *The Hobbit*. Then, when the first draft of *LOTR* was complete, he went back and changed *The Hobbit* to make the two books fit together better.

Most of the changes are in the chapter in which Bilbo meets Gollum and finds the Ring. The changes make the Ring seem much more important to Gollum. They also show how it has made him evil. For example:

—The new Gollum values the Ring more. He doesn't offer the Ring as a prize, as in the first version. It's too important to risk. Instead, he offers Bilbo a way out of the cave.

—The new Gollum is more cunning. Bilbo sees that he is tricky and would do anything to keep the Ring. But in the first version, Gollum is willing to let Bilbo have the Ring as a matter of honor, after their riddle contest.

—The new Gollum is more attached to the Ring. He seems to go crazy as soon as he

The actor who helped create the animated Gollum for the *LOTR* films imagined that the Ring is a drug, and Gollum is an addict who craves it despite its evil effects. It makes sense for showing how Gollum behaves. But Tolkien was not thinking about addicts when he created Gollum.

realizes he has lost it. (He doesn't know Bilbo has it.) In the first version, he just gets confused.

—The new Gollum is more dangerous. He thinks about eating Bilbo instead of letting him leave the cave. But in the first version, he actually apologizes to Bilbo for not being able to give the promised prize.

—The Ring itself is also different. In the original, it simply makes the wearer invisible. In the new version, Tolkien calls it a "ring of power."

It's almost hard to recognize that original Gollum. All that effort to keep his word! In the new version, however, he is suddenly the

"Gollum ultimately has to break your heart. He's not merely a villain—you have to feel for him."

—Mark Ordesky, executive producer of the *LOTR* films.

creature we know. Tolkien scholar Bonniejean Christensen, who first pointed to the differences between the two versions, puts it well: Gollum becomes a "withered, totally depraved creature dominated by an evil ring and capable of any crime."

Tolkien explains away the two different versions in *LOTR*'s prologue, with an excuse that neatly fits the story to follow. He says the earlier version was a lie Bilbo told, probably due to the Ring's influence. The later version only became known after Gandalf scared the truth out of Bilbo. Pretty clever of Tolkien to make it fit together that way, isn't it? And the new Gollum is so much more interesting than the first.

See also:

Baggins, Bilbo
Riddles
Rings

WHAT NIGHTMARE HAUNTED GONDOR?

EVER HAD A dream so bad it woke you? Tolkien did. In fact, one bad dream came to him again and again, starting when he was a child and continuing through adulthood.

Instead of just being frightened by it, he tried to understand it. The dream became an obsession: he drew pictures of it; he composed poems about it. But those efforts, by his own account, weren't enough to solve the puzzle.

Eventually he found a way. The dream led him to write a story about the early

65

years of Middle-earth, and the story became the background of some important characters in *LOTR*.

HERE COMES THE FLOOD

Tolkien said
Númenóreans
who survived to
live in Gondor are
like ancient
Egyptians. They
admire huge
buildings and
statues, like the
pyramids and the
Great Sphinx in
Egypt. They build
elaborate tombs.
Even the crowns
of their kings
resemble the tall
crowns of
Egyptian royalty.

The nightmare Tolkien suffered was always the same. A great wave would mysteriously appear out of the ocean, or rush over land. Each time, panic woke Tolkien from the dream. He lay in bed gasping, as if he had been drowning.

The more Tolkien thought about this dream, the more he was drawn to old stories of worlds destroyed by a great wave. This is a common legend, from ancient folk tales to the Bible story of Noah's Ark and the great flood. Tolkien eventually went back to one of the most famous: the story of the lost island of Atlantis.

The Greek philosopher Plato set down the Atlantis story 2400 years ago. According to him, the events had happened perhaps 7000 years earlier. Supposedly, Atlantis was a large island in the Atlantic Ocean, home to a magnificent civilization founded by the sea god Poseidon. The humans who lived there were gifted with extraordinary knowledge and skills. As Plato writes:

For many generations, as long as their divine nature lasted, they were obedient to the rule of laws, and revered the god who gave them life. They had great spirits, uniting gentleness with wisdom in their outlook and relations with one another. They despised everything but virtue, thinking lightly of the possession of gold and other property, which seemed only a burden to them. Neither were they intoxicated by luxury; nor did wealth deprive them of their self-control.

Sadly, the Atlanteans' paradise did not last. "Their divine character began to fade away, and human nature got the upper hand," says Plato. "They believed themselves to be glorious and blessed at the very time when they were full of greed and unrighteous power." Hoping to become an empire, Atlantis waged war against the great Greek city, Athens. This angered the god Zeus. Deciding to punish the Atlanteans, he sank their island beneath the ocean.

Beginning a few hundred years ago, scholars began to theorize that Atlantis was not a lost island in the ocean but rather a lost civilization. There are now theories placing it in nearly every spot on the globe.

TOLKIEN'S ATLANTIS

Over the years, storytellers have added every possible twist to the Atlantis legend. Tolkien, however, stays very close to Plato's version. In his version, Atlantis is known as Númenor. It is given to certain humans for helping the Elves in a war. These humans have many fine qualities, but are tricked by Sauron and become evil. As a result, the God of Middle-earth sends a great wave to wash away their home island and sink their warships. The few virtuous humans who survive the wave end up in Middle-earth, where some of them establish Gondor. Aragorn is one their descendants, as are Boromir and Faramir.

WASH AWAY YOUR TEARS

Tolkien believed Plato's legend was based on an actual event. More than that, he believed his nightmare was a real memory inherited from an ancestor who had lived through the flood thousands of years earlier. (If that seems odd, consider this: he later learned one of his sons often had the same dream.) In *LOTR*, Faramir seems to have inherited the nightmare in the same way, from his Númenórean ancestors.

By writing about Númenor, Tolkien was

trying to imagine history as it really happened. Whether or not he did that, the effort to understand his nightmare had a completely unexpected side effect: he stopped having it.

WHAT'S THE ORIGIN OF THE WORD "HOBBIT"?

Hobbits

READERS SCRATCHED THEIR heads in wonder. As soon as *The Hobbit* appeared in 1937, they began to guess the origin of the title. Though they couldn't find the word in a dictionary, some were sure they'd heard it before. Because hobbits are small, have furry feet, and live underground, many readers were certain Tolkien had combined "human" and "rabbit." One thought the creatures and their name came from an African legend.

Those guesses, and almost all the others like them, were wrong.

The fact is, the word came to Tolkien in a flash, and it was some time before even he pieced together the many sources behind that moment of inspiration.

DAYDREAM BELIEVER

The word came to him at an unlikely time. He was marking exam papers—a task that bored him. Naturally his attention wandered. While daydreaming for a moment, he wrote a sentence on a blank page in a student's exam book. The line would become the opening of his novel: "In a hole in the ground there lived a hobbit" (*The Hobbit* by J.R.R. Tolkien, 3).

For a professor of Old English, the word "hobbit" makes sense in that sentence. It's almost a joke, because the Old English words for "hole dweller" are *hol bytla*. So of course a hobbit would live in a hole.

But there was more behind it, as Tolkien later came to realize.

CHASING RABBITS

Tolkien always said "hobbits" have nothing to do with rabbits. He said their size and shape were an effort to please his children, who liked creatures called "Snergs" in one of their books, *The Marvellous Land of Snergs* by E. A. Wyke-Smith. The Snergs are "only slightly taller than the average table but broad in the shoulders and of great strength." Tolkien told one friend that *Snergs* "was probably an unconscious source-book for the Hobbits" (*Tolkien* by H. Carpenter, 165).

The word "hobbit" is supposedly just a translation by Tolkien, for our sake, from the language Westron (Common Speech), which hobbits used. Their word for themselves is actually "kuduk."

However, Thomas Shippey, a linguistics expert and Tolkien biographer, insists "rabbit" is probably part of the story, at least subconsciously, because of the many times Bilbo is called a rabbit or a bunny by other characters, such as the Trolls, Beorn, and an Eagle. Bilbo even thinks of himself as one when the Eagles are coming to get him; and he shakes like one when Thorin is angry at him (*The Road to Middle-earth* by T. A. Shippey, 52).

BORN IN THE U.S.A.?

Some readers who made a long-shot guess at the word's origin, on the basis of sound alone, may have been close to the mark. A well-known 1922 novel entitled *Babbitt*, by Sinclair Lewis, tells of a suburban American who gets bored with his comfortable life and becomes slightly adventurous—just like Bilbo Baggins, the hero of *The Hobbit*, who gets bored with the limited life in the Shire. Tolkien himself thought there was a connection here.

Digging out of a Hole

Still, these bits of explanation didn't satisify every reader. Some were certain the word had more of a history. In time, professionals joined the hunt. In 1970, the editors of the *Oxford English Dictionary* (on which Tolkien had worked fifty years earlier), decided to include the word, and were determined to find its source. They searched through old literature for evidence, which they sent to Tolkien. Perhaps it was related to "hob," a word for a "country type" or "clown" that goes back to the 1300s? Or maybe "hobgoblin"? Tolkien didn't think so. Then a sharp researcher found an 1895 book that says, "The whole earth was overrun with ghosts, boggles . . . hobbits, hobgoblins." But Tolkien had never read that book, as best as he could remember. In the end, the *OED* decided to credit Tolkien with the first use of the word to mean the friendly, hole-dwelling creatures we know and love.

All this may seem like a lot of fuss over one little word, and readers who devote their time to this sort of investigation may seem a little eccentric. But you have to admit: it's just the sort of thing Tolkien would have done.

See also:

Names

WHICH
LANGUAGE
LAUNCHED
TOLKIEN?

Languages

HAVE YOU EVER been caught reading Tolkien when you had other work to do? Take heart: if Tolkien had been a more attentive student, he might never have written *LOTR*. A major inspiration for his stories is an obscure language he discovered while avoiding schoolwork.

STUDY BREAK

By the time he entered Oxford University, Tolkien had already invented a handful of languages, and extra words for real ones. One day in the college library, while he was supposed to be studying for exams, he came across a grammar book for a language that interested him more than all the others. He later said it was the "rocket" that

75

launched his stories (*The Letters of J.R.R. Tolkien* edited by H. Carpenter with C. Tolkien, 214).

The language was Finnish. It became the strongest influence on his invented languages, especially Quenya (High-elven). Just as important, it sent him back to a Finnish epic poem he had read years earlier in English translation. Rereading it in the original language, he felt the urge to write a similar epic for England. In time, he borrowed many references from it for his own stories.

PEOPLE WITHOUT A PAST

The Finnish epic is called the *Kalevala*. It is a collection of songs, poems, stories, and magical charms that were passed down by folk

An 1847 cartoon shows Elias Lönnrot on a trip to collect folk tales in the countryside. The caption said, "A single man, scurrying about, has created a heritage for us."

singers until a student of languages wrote them down in the 1830s and 1840s.

The story of its creation has fascinating parallels with Tolkien's work. Although the *Kalevala* is now commonly described as the "national epic" of Finland, when it was written Finland was not much of a nation. Modern Finland achieved independence less than a hundred years ago, in 1917. (That was three years *after* Tolkien found the grammar book.) For most of the seven centuries before, it had been ruled either by its neighbor to the west, Sweden, or its neighbor to the east, Russia. Its cultural identity was sketchy.

About a hundred years before Tolkien began writing *LOTR*, Finnish academics began to think folk tales could renew the Finnish identity, so they began to collect them. The greatest contribution to this effort was made by Elias Lönnrot (1802–84). Over two decades he collected much of the *Kalevala*, arranged the chapters, and even named it. (*Kalevala* means "Kaleva's District." A man named Kaleva was said to be the first settler in Finland, and its first hero.)

February 28, the anniversary of the day of the *Kalevala's* first publication in 1835, is celebrated as Kalevala Day in Finland.

THE *KALEVALA* AND TOLKIEN

This passion for Finnish—first Lönnrot's, then Tolkien's—was the spark for Tolkien's work. Tolkien stated plainly that his stories of early Middle-earth began as an effort to rewrite and improve upon the *Kalevala*. Eventually he borrowed many details from it.

Names. In part because Finnish and High-elven are similar, names from the *Kalevala* echo in Tolkien's works. For example, the God of Tolkien's world is named Ilúvatar. *The Silmarillion*, Tolkien's legends of the First Age, begins by describing Ilúvatar's creation of the world. The *Kalevala* begins with the story of Ilmatar, the spirit who shapes the earth.

Themes. A magical object in the *Kalevala* relates to the One Ring of *LOTR*. In the Finnish epic, Ilmarinen, the blacksmith of the gods, forges the Sampo—a mill that grinds out endless amounts of grain, salt, and money, leading to enormous wealth and power. Just as forging the One Ring was difficult for Sauron, creating the Sampo was difficult even for Ilmarinen, who forged the heavens. As he works, many great objects emerge from the furnace—a magic crossbow, a magic ship, a magic boat, a magic plow—but none are good enough. Ilmarinen puts them all back in the fire. Finally:

On the third night Ilmarinen,
Bending low to view his metals,

On the bottom of the furnace,
Sees the magic Sampo rising,
Sees the lid in many colors.
Quick the artist of Wainola
Forges with the tongs and anvil,
Knocking with a heavy hammer,
Forges skilfully the Sampo;
On one side the flour is grinding,
On another salt is making,
On a third is money forging,
And the lid is many-colored.

Tolkien began working on Quenya in 1915, when he was just twenty-three years old, and it soon had a vocabulary of hundreds of words. Now it has many more. People have written whole poems in Quenya.

But soon the Sampo becomes a source of trouble. A bitter rivalry develops between two regions over its ownership. The effect of the Sampo is like that of the One Ring, which causes moral corruption and fierce war.

Stories. Tolkien adapted whole stories from the *Kalevala* for his mythology. He was especially interested in the story of the evil Kullervo, using him as the model for a character in *The Silmarillion* named Túrin Turambar ("Master of Doom"). Both men are outlaws; both accidentally fall in love with their sisters, after which both sisters kill themselves; both seek revenge repeatedly, with only tragic results; and, finally, both end their lives by speaking to their swords, asking their swords to kill them.

A MODERN MYTHOLOGY

Names, characters, themes, stories—echoes of all these things in the *Kalevala* can be found in Tolkien's work. Yet the most important inspiration for Tolkien was knowing that someone else had succeeded at an idea he wanted to try. He said often his novels rose from a desire to create myths for England. By that, he meant he wanted to fill a gap in literary history. Before the Anglo-Saxons arrived in England from Europe in the fifth century, Britain was mostly Celtic. We still enjoy Celtic myths, like the tales of King Arthur. But they didn't satisfy Tolkien's interest in his Anglo-Saxon ancestors. Unfortunately, Anglo-Saxon myths aren't much better, because they are more about Europe than England. (*Beowulf*, for example, is about Scandinavia.) Tolkien wanted Anglo-Saxon tales that take place in England.

Lönnrot's work on the *Kalevala* showed Tolkien that a student of languages can build a modern mythology from an assortment of legends. Typical of Tolkien, it was a lesson he learned when he was supposed to be studying something else.

See also:

Names

HOW MANY LANGUAGES DID TOLKIEN INVENT?

YOU AND YOUR friends may have spoken Pig Latin, or invented secret words that only you understood. Tolkien also played with words. As a child, he created languages of his own. Later, studying languages became his profession, and he continued to invent new ones. He even traced his work as a novelist back to his desire to create languages. To make a language work, he says in several letters and interviews, it must have stories to tell. So he wrote the stories.

"NEW NONSENSE"

Tolkien's fascination with foreign words appeared early. As a child, he was charmed by the Welsh names he saw on coal trucks.

The languages
Tolkien knew
included: Ancient
Greek, Latin,
Gothic, Old Norse
(Old Icelandic),
Swedish,
Norwegian,
Danish, Anglo-
Saxon (Old
English), Middle
English, German,
Dutch, French,
Spanish, Italian,
Welsh, and
Finnish.

When he was a teenager he learned that his interest was shared by two younger cousins, who had invented a language called Animalic, based on animal names. Tolkien learned it quickly, and then created a new language with one of the cousins. They called it Nevbosh, which means "New Nonsense." It was a hodgepodge of English, French, and Latin— more of a private joke than an ordered system. His next attempt, Naffarin, was more organized. It was based heavily on Spanish, thanks to the Spanish guardian who cared for him.

Then Tolkien came across Gothic, an old European language that fascinated him for years. No one speaks Gothic now, but because it's so old, it helps explain many languages that followed, including old forms of English and German. For fun, Tolkien created new Gothic words from pieces of old ones.

He dropped Gothic when he came across Finnish, which was also obscure at the time. (Finland wasn't yet an independent country. Many Finns spoke Swedish.) Tolkien was spellbound by Finnish grammar. Soon after finding a book on the subject, he began to invent Quenya, his High-elven language that is so important to *LOTR*.

WORKING WITH WORDS

By this time, Tolkien knew he would become a university professor of languages. Even the army service that interrupted his career was focused on languages. He specialized in communications, learning Morse code and other methods of the time.

For his academic studies, he chose Anglo-Saxon (Old English). He felt a connection with it, which he believed was the result of having Anglo-Saxon ancestors.

In 1919 and 1920, he helped write the *Oxford English Dictionary*, which he said was the greatest learning experience of his career.

One of the languages Tolkien had to learn for the army was semaphore—actually an alphabet, made by holding flags a certain way. It was used to spell out messages across long distances before radios were common.

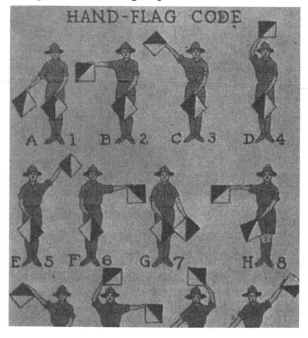

By the time
Tolkien began
working on the
the *Oxford
English
Dictionary*, the
project was up to
the letter "W."
Among his
assigned words
were "warm,"
"wasp," "water,"
and "winter." The
sources he found
for those words
can still be found
in the dictionary.

The supervisor of the project was greatly impressed with his talent: "His work gives evidence of an unusually thorough mastery of Anglo-Saxon and of the facts and principles of the comparative grammar of the Germanic languages. Indeed, I have no hesitation in saying that I have never known a man of his age who was in these respects his equal" (*Tolkien* by H. Carpenter, 101).

HIS LANGUAGES AND HIS NOVELS

Most writers spend time trying to find the right word, but Tolkien's focus on language was much more intense. He often stopped writing a story to work out the history of a word, even though he knew it wouldn't mean much to anyone but him. He had to get it right before he could continue with the story.

One reason for all the work is that Tolkien wanted his invented languages to mimic real languages in a certain way. He knew that real languages influence each other by sharing words and grammar as their speakers mix together. He wanted the languages of Middle-earth to show the same kind of development according to Middle-earth's history. The relationship between Quenya (High-elven) and Sindarin (Grey-elven) is a good example. Quenya is the early language of the Elves, which Tolkien sometimes refers to in letters as Elven-Latin. Just as Latin is considered out of date in our world, except for ceremonies such as school assemblies or the Catholic Mass, by the time of Frodo's adventure in *LOTR*, Quenya is used mostly for formal occasions in Middle-earth. Sindarin is used by the Grey Elves (Sindar) of Middle-earth. Tolkien intends the relationship of Quenya to Sindarin to be the same as Latin's relationship to the Celtic and Welsh languages used in Britain when the Romans arrived. This fits the history of Sindarin in Tolkien's mythology: it is more native to Middle-earth than Quenya. But bits of Quenya have slipped into Sindarin, just as Latin slipped into the languages of Britain.

Tolkien believed the sound of each invented language is linked to the character of the people who speak it. For instance, both High-elven (Quenya) and Grey-elven (Sindarin) are based on languages he found beautiful (Finnish and Welsh). This fits his warm feelings about Elves. Meanwhile, the Black Speech, used by Sauron and his followers in Mordor, has an awful sound.

THE ABCs OF MIDDLE-EARTH

Just as he created languages, Tolkien invented alphabets. Some of them are related to real ancient alphabets in our world.

On Middle-earth there are two basic types of writing. The *Tengwar* ("letters") are written script, such as the writing on the Ring. The *Cirth* ("runes") are scratched or carved.

Runes were very familiar to Tolkien, given his training in Old English. They were the first alphabet used in northern Europe, appearing in the third century A.D., and were used for more than a thousand years. They can still be found in Britain, Scandinavia, and Iceland. The name comes from the Gaelic word *rûn* ("secret"). They are said to be a gift from the gods. According to one story, the Norse god Odin hangs himself for nine days from Yggdrasil, the great ash tree that holds earth, heaven, and hell, until he finally understands the runes. His effort is supposed to

Runes on a granite block in Sweden, dating back to the age of the Vikings.

show the value of knowledge. When runes were first used, any knowledge of reading and writing was rare. Those who understood runes were considered wizards, and were often asked to use the runes to see the future. This is also true in *LOTR*. Gandalf's knowledge of runes impresses the other members of the Fellowship.

WORD TO THE WISE

Experts disagree about the precise number of languages Tolkien invented for Middle-earth. The differing opinions are due to different definitions. Does it count as a language if Tolkien merely created a handful of words for it? What if he referred to it in a history written long after *LOTR*?

Tolkien expert Ruth S. Noel counts "at least fourteen" invented languages in *LOTR*. Helge Kåre Fauskanger, another expert, finds fragments of, and references to, several more—perhaps as many as twenty-one.

Tolkien knew these invented languages would mystify many readers. More than once he commented that it was odd for him to spend so much time worrying about those details. However, not being particularly concerned about the opinions of others, he continued to satisfy himself. In fact, he could

A rune shaped like our modern letter "y" has the sound "th," and is the origin of signs like "YE OLDE SHOPPE." The correct pronunciation of "Ye" in this case is no different from "The."

See also:

Names

not stop. Merely inventing characters and telling the story did not fulfil his desire to create. Few other writers would feel the need to invent languages for their characters; but for Tolkien, it was an essential part of storytelling.

COULD MIDDLE-EARTH BE MORE MAGICAL?

Magic

Far too many people try to compare J.R.R. Tolkien and J. K. Rowling, just because both of them tell stories about imaginary worlds inhabited by wizards. Not much about their stories is similar. Harry Potter lives in a world full of magic: spells, wands, potions, and flying broomsticks. In Tolkien's world, the wizards (and others) of Middle-earth perform very little magic. In fact, Tolkien denies that magic is important in his world. He made a point of saying that he uses the word "wizard" to mean something "utterly distinct from Sorcerer or Magician" (*The Letters of J.R.R. Tolkien* edited by H. Carpenter with C. Tolkien, 159).

However, examples of magic do exist in his books. Among them:

—The Ring makes the wearer invisible.

—Aragorn knows how to use the healing plant athelas ("kingsfoil").

—The palantíri (seeing-stones) allow one to magically see across space and time.

Some of these examples are crucial to the plot. How does Tolkien explain them?

With all due respect to Tolkien, he doesn't answer the question clearly. In a letter written after *LOTR* was published, Tolkien worries that he is "too casual" about referring to magic in the book, and especially about terming it "magic" at all. The question, he says, is "v[ery] difficult" (*The Letters of J.R.R. Tolkien* edited by H. Carpenter with C. Tolkien, 199).

One problem is that *LOTR* is told from the point of view of hobbits. As Tolkien says in the prologue, "Hobbits have never, in fact, studied magic of any kind" (*The Lord of the Rings* by J.R.R. Tolkien, 1). They don't know very much about Elves or humans, either. So what appears as magic to them—such as Aragorn's ability to heal—might be superior knowledge rather than actual enchantment. Even Galadriel fails to understand why the

The Ring's power to make its wearer invisible comes from Tolkien's favorite fairy tale as a child. In that story, the hero Sigurd wears a magic gold helmet that makes him invisible, while trying to win a ring cursed by a dwarf much like Gollum (See **Gollum**).

hobbits think Elves are magical, as she tells Sam when showing him her Mirror.

Also, some characters, like Gandalf and Saruman, who appear to use magical spells, were actually created as supernatural beings by Ilúvatar, the God of Tolkien's world. Their God-given gifts are something quite different from magic.

These explanations don't cover every case, because Tolkien developed the philosophy behind Middle-earth over time, not as part of

Aragorn's ability to heal with what seems to be magic is shared by other kings in legend, including Charlemagne and Arthur. It was considered a divine gift.

a plan. It's not fair to expect him to be perfect. However, you can generally assume Tolkien wanted to limit the magic in Middle-earth. He didn't want characters to build towers with one wave of a magic wand, or to fly to Mount Doom by sprinkling fairy dust. He wanted life in Middle-earth to be hard. He wanted the Fellowship's mission to destroy the One Ring to be tough and dangerous. That's what makes it worthwhile.

See also:

Gandalf

WHERE IN THE WORLD IS MIDDLE-EARTH?

WE CAN SETTLE one fact right away: Middle-earth is not an imaginary place, like Oz or Lilliput. It is not a planet in outer space. It is not in the Earth's core.

Middle-earth is Europe. The name simply comes from the Middle English term *Middel-erthe*—the name Europeans called their land many hundreds of years ago.

True, Tolkien's maps and descriptions of Middle-earth don't follow all the features of modern Europe—for instance, neither the shape of Britain nor today's Atlantic coast are obvious on his maps. As he says in the prologue to *LOTR*, those features don't match exactly because they changed over time. Still, there's no doubt about a few points of origin. Hobbiton is located—not surprisingly—near

Tolkien estimated that Frodo's adventure in *LOTR* took place about 6000 years ago, by our calendar.

93

Tolkien's home, in Oxford. Gondor is roughly where we now find Italy, though it may extend as far as Turkey.

NEVER THE TWAIN SHALL MEET

If the location of *LOTR* seems ordinary, don't be disappointed. Geography is a big influence on the plot, but in less obvious ways.

Tolkien believed that over the course of history, different directions come to mean different things. In England, for instance, east came to be connected with enemies and danger, because of invasions by Scandinavians to the east. Tolkien matches the meaning of the directions in *LOTR* with the meanings from real European history and legend.

South. In the real ancient world, heading south from Britain sent you towards great empires: Greece, Rome, Byzantium. The same is true in *LOTR*. Gondor, where humans reign over a great kingdom, is south of Hobbiton, and quite close to those real-life places. South is the direction of civilization, of large nations and complicated politics, as the hobbits learn when they reach Gondor.

North. No surprise here: in legends of northern Europe, the icy north is associated with death. It is where one finds Niflheim, a place of everlasting cold and night, where

The "Black Land" of Middle-earth, Sauron's empire of Mordor, is located where you now find the Black Sea.

unworthy souls go after death. As a line in
an Icelandic saga goes, "Cold arose out of
Niflheim, and all terrible things." This land
is the source of *LOTR*'s "Region of Everlasting Cold," home of the leader of the Black
Riders.

West. For Europeans, west was the direction of mystery, because the vast Atlantic
Ocean stood in the way of exploration. Legends grew of magical lands beyond the sea
and the people who lived there. The legend of
the lost island of Atlantis, an important inspiration for Tolkien, grew from this fascination.
According to some stories, people from those
lands had crossed the sea to settle in Europe.
Tolkien used that idea to explain how certain
humans came to Middle-earth and established
Gondor. He also relied on these legends when
writing about the Undying Lands, part of the
home of the angelic spirits.

East. Early in *LOTR*, Gandalf tells Frodo
to begin his journey by heading east, "towards
danger" (*The Lord of the Rings* by J.R.R.
Tolkien, 65). Bilbo Baggins also headed east
in *The Hobbit*, towards a frightening forest
and the mountains where Orcs live. For the
hobbits of Middle-earth, as for western Europeans in real life, east came to mean danger
because that's where foreign enemies and

armies lived. Of course, it's also where one finds Sauron's realm, Mordor.

HERE, THERE, AND EVERYWHERE

The four points of the compass don't mean the same things to people in every part of the world. In China, for example, enemies tended to invade from the north and west. That's why the Great Wall was built along the northern border. Even in western Europe, traditional meanings are changing. Technology such as jet planes and cell phones make distances on a map seem shorter than in Tolkien's day. The faraway land across the Atlantic is no longer mysterious: it's just America. The same pop songs play in Moscow and Paris. A Scandinavian invasion of England usually involves a football match, and is over by the last flight home of the weekend.

However, landscape still shapes history and culture. New legends are sure to arise. Even if the next fantasy epic you read spans the entire globe, rather than just the old *Middel-erthe*, a sense of direction will mean something to the story.

Every culture likes to think it sits in the center of the world. Just as Europeans called their land *Middel-erthe*, the Chinese call their land *Chung-kuo*, meaning "Middle Kingdom."

HOW DID TOLKIEN NAME NAMES?

TOLKIEN SPENT HIS life pulling words apart to discover how they work. You can learn a lot by doing the same to his words, especially names.

CAUGHT IN A WEB OF WORDS

Quite often, Tolkien created names from roots of old words he found while studying languages. One simple example is the giant spider, Shelob. In Old English, *lob* means "spider"; so Tolkien gives us "she-lob" for a female spider. Sometimes he pulled names from old texts. For example, confusing forests called "Mirkwood" appear in many old stories. "Woses," the name of the wild humans of Middle-earth, is a shortening of *wodwos*, an Old English term for legendary wild men of

Tolkien pronounced his name *Toll-keen,* not *Toll-kin.*

the forest. Many names in *The Hobbit* come from a list of dwarves in an Old Norse poem. "Gandalf"—which means "sorcerer elf"—comes from the same list.

Tolkien also borrowed from what he found around him, especially when creating the landscape of Middle-earth. Tolkien expert Thomas Shippey says: "Five minutes with the *Oxford Dictionary of Place-Names*, E. Ekwall's *English River Names* or P. H. Reaney's *Dictionary of British Surnames* will provide explanations for most hobbitic names of any sort, and the same is true, on a more learned scale, of the rest of Middle-earth. Thus Celeborn's 'Wetwang' is also a place in Yorkshire, the Riders' 'Dunharrow' has evident English parallels, the rivers Gladden, Silverlode, Limlight, etc., all have English roots . . ." (*The Road to Middle-earth* by T. A. Shippey, 78–9).

"Tolkien" comes from the German word for "foolhardy." Supposedly, it was given to the family after a daring military escapade by one of Tolkien's ancestors. Tolkien wasn't convinced the story was true, and didn't think the name described him.

AND BINGO WAS HIS NAME-O

In some cases, names came to Tolkien in a flash. At times, however, tinkering was needed. The best example of a name that came slowly may be "Frodo." Our hero's original name was sillier, fitting his hobbit origins. He was called "Bingo Bolger-Baggins." (It almost makes him sound like Tigger from A. A. Milne's *Winnie the Pooh*, bouncing to Mount

Doom on springs.) "The Bingos" was the name his children gave to their favorite stuffed animals, some toy koala bears.

Tolkien wrote quite a bit of *LOTR* using "Bingo Bolger-Baggins," and resisted changing it even when he sensed it didn't fit. But as the tone of *LOTR* grew more serious, he realized he had to drop it. Fortunately, a better name was at hand. He had already given the name "Frodo" to one of Bingo's traveling companions. That name, Tolkien knew, has a noble origin. Mentioned briefly in the Anglo-Saxon epic *Beowulf,* it refers to a king in a Norse saga. (The spelling is "Fródi" in Old Norse.)

Fródi was crowned king in the time when Augustus Caesar [emperor of Rome] imposed peace on all the world—at the time Christ was born. But because Fródi was mightiest of all kings in the Northern lands, the peace was called by his name wherever Danish was spoken: "the Peace of Fródi." No man injured another, even though he met face to face his father's slayer or his brother's. Nor was any man thief nor robber, so that a gold ring lay untouched for years on Jalangr's Heath.

Tolkien loved to make up funny names from strange phrases he found. A sign reading "BILL STICKERS WILL BE PROSECUTED" led to family stories about a "Bill Stickers." Other stories described a former military man with a name from a street sign: "Major Road Ahead."

Would you
believe Aragorn
began life as a
hobbit? The
character
appeared to
Tolkien suddenly,
well into the
writing of *LOTR*,
as a strange
hobbit named
"Trotter." For a
long time, Tolkien
worried that he
would never
figure out the
identity of the
secretive stranger.
But eventually the
hobbit became a
human, and
"Trotter" became
"Strider."

The parallels to Tolkien's story are obvious: both the Icelandic king and Tolkien's Frodo seek to establish peace, and their examples are so great their people resist the temptation of a golden ring. Tolkien even drops a line from the Norse saga into *LOTR*: speaking about the Ring, Faramir tells Frodo twice that he would not take the Ring if he found it lying by the road (*The Lord of the Rings* by J.R.R. Tolkien, 656, 665).

As well as these connections in legend, Tolkien liked the name's meaning: "the wise one." So his Ring-bearer became "Frodo."

Other names offer examples of Tolkien's various sources:

Bag End (as in "Baggins of Bag End"). One of Tolkien's aunts lived at the end of a road that locals called Bag End. It's a deliberately unsnobby (and therefore hobbit-like) way to say cul-de-sac ("end of the bag"), which means "dead end." (Bilbo's pretentious Sackville-Baggins relatives put the fancy phrase back in their name.)

Crack of Doom. This term, which Tolkien knew from Shakespeare's *Macbeth* among other sources, refers to a signal—a crack of thunder or a blast of trumpets—marking the arrival of the Last Judgment, as told in the Bible. Tolkien turned it into an actual crack, a fissure in Mount Doom where the Ring must be destroyed. (As scholar Ruth S. Noel says, Frodo's effort to reach the Crack of Doom is like a Judgment Day for Middle-earth.)

Gamgee, Samwise. The last name is from Dr. Samuel Gamgee, inventor of Gamgee Tissue, an absorbent cotton used in medicine. He was a local hero in Birmingham before Tolkien moved there as a child. "Samwise" is Old English for "half-wise" or "half-wit." It describes Sam as we first meet him, not the truly wise companion he becomes.

Mark. The land of the Riders of the Mark comes from Mercia, the Anglo-Saxon kingdom in the area of Birmingham and Oxford.

Misty Mountains. This phrase is borrowed from Norse legends. It suggests a place that is full of dangers hidden in the half-darkness. (It's the mountain version of "Mirkwood.")

Mordor. This name for Sauron's realm, meaning "Black Land" in Tolkien's invented Grey-elven language, comes from the Old English *morthor*, meaning "mortal sin" or "murder."

Nazg. This word, meaning "ring" in Black Speech, appears on the inscription of the One Ring and in a name of the Black Riders, "Nazgûl" ("ring wraith" or "ring ghoul"). In our world, it is the Gaelic word for "ring."

In 1973, *The Hobbit* was translated into Icelandic, one of Tolkien's favorite languages. This pleased him greatly. He commented that Icelandic would suit the story better than any other language. Many of the names he used, such as "Gandalf," were drawn from Old Norse (Old Icelandic).

Surprisingly, Tolkien forgot that fact—at least consciously—until long after finishing *LOTR*.

Rohan. This is the name of a famous family in France. The family's history involves politics and war, but Tolkien just liked the word. He wasn't making a point by using it.

Saruman. From the Old English *searu*, which means "tricky" or "cunning."

Sauron. From an Old Norse word meaning "detestable" or "abominable."

WHAT'S IN A NAME?

Tolkien saw all these names as puzzles. He enjoyed working on them, even though they didn't move the plot forward. Referring to the names of places, Thomas Shippey says the time Tolkien spent "seems largely wasted," because not all the names are important to the story (*The Road to Middle-earth* by T. A. Shippey, 78–9). But they did serve a purpose, Shippey adds. The maps and names help make Middle-earth seem more real.

What Shippey says about the place-names is also true of the names of people and things. All of them give *LOTR* the appearance of real history, just as Tolkien intended.

Tolkien and his brother picked *bilberries* near their childhood home outside Birmingham— perhaps the word was an inspiration for Bilbo's name.

See also:

Ents

Hobbits

Languages

Orcs

HOW DID ORCS GET SO UGLY?

Orcs

MANY OF THE nasty creatures who serve Sauron and Saruman work and live in a fiery, underground hell. That suits them perfectly. It's not only their origin according to the history of Middle-earth; it's also their origin in Tolkien's imagination.

Their name comes from the Roman god of the underworld, Orcus, which is also the Latin word for Hell itself. Tolkien wasn't the first to use it to describe monsters. An Old English form of it, meaning "ogre" or "hell-demon," appears in *Beowulf*. For a long time, it described a sea monster, as in this account from a legend about a knight of King Charlemagne: "The horrible monster was like nothing that nature produces. It was but one

The poet William Blake (1757–1827) also used the name Orc. In the mythology he created, Orc is the rebellious child of two of the first spirits.

mass of tossing and twisting body, with nothing of the animal but head, eyes, and mouth, the last furnished with tusks like those of the wild boar." That Orc was probably based on stories of killer whales, which now have the Latin name *Orcinus orca*.

Tolkien's Orcs are more like the dwarves of legend. They first appear in *The Hobbit*, as "goblins." Tolkien was inspired by creatures in stories by George Macdonald, an author of popular fantasy novels written a few decades before Tolkien was born. In *The Princess and the Goblin*, Macdonald introduces his version:

The sea monster Orc (*orca* in Latin) pictured in an engraving from 1539.

There was a legend current in the country that at one time they lived above ground, and were very like other people. But for some reason or other they had all taken refuge in the subterranean caverns, whence they never came out but at night. . . .

[T]hey had greatly altered in the course of generations; and no wonder, seeing they lived away from the sun, in cold and wet and dark places. They were not ordinarily ugly, but either absolutely hideous, or ludicrously grotesque both in face and form. . . . And as they grew misshapen in body they had grown in knowledge and cleverness, and now were able to do things no mortal could see the possibility of. But as they grew in cunning, they grew in mischief . . . and they had strength equal to their cunning.

In the end, Macdonald's goblins prove to be not all that bad, and easily outwitted. Tolkien's goblins in *The Hobbit* are also defeated easily.

For *LOTR*, Tolkien created goblins far

Macdonald's goblins are famous for having a particular weakness: tender feet. Tolkien ignored that part of the story on purpose.

more disgusting than Macdonald ever imagined. But he kept one feature that goes back to the same legends that originally inspired Macdonald. Orcs start out as another species, then become misshapen over time, as they live underground. They are like demons shaped by the fires of hell. Tolkien made that old idea fit his own history of Middle-earth's early years: in his version, Sauron's master, Melkor, the first Dark Lord, bred the Orcs out of Elves he had captured and put in underground prisons, using "slow arts of cruelty" to change the Elves into Orcs (*The Silmarillion* by J.R.R. Tolkien, 50). So Orcs look gruesome because of how Melkor made them. And we can probably guess that he liked them that way.

See also:

Elves

Sauron

Silmarillion, The

DO HOBBITS
BELIEVE IN
GOD?

Religion

WITH ALL THE great forces at work in the battle over the Ring, you might wonder why
Frodo never prays for help from the most
powerful force of all. In fact, there's almost no
prayer or other ritual in *LOTR*. You could
read the entire book and wonder whether
Tolkien or his creatures believed in God. But
without a doubt, there's a lot of religion in
LOTR. Tolkien says it is "a fundamentally religious and Catholic work" (*The Letters of
J.R.R. Tolkien* edited by H. Carpenter with
C. Tolkien, 172). So why doesn't anyone ask
for God's help to defeat Sauron?

Tolkien wanted the book to show
religion, rather than talk about it.
When Frodo is merciful to Gollum,
despite every temptation to act

otherwise, he shows Tolkien's belief in compassion and forgiveness. When Frodo presses on towards Mount Doom despite nagging worries, he shows Tolkien's belief in trusting a divine plan. Other characters display the same qualities and face the same tests.

Major themes also show religious ideas. The pain and regret Elves feel because they have to live forever shows that, in Tolkien's view, humans are lucky to be free from that worry. When Melkor and Sauron try to act like gods in Middle-earth, they always fall short of actually creating something original, and have to deform something made by God, such as when they make Orcs out of Elves. Only the one God, Ilúvatar, can create.

Tolkien's religion influences every page of *LOTR*. If you don't notice it, don't worry: that's just what Tolkien intended. He wanted to be subtle. He even built the lack of religious ceremony into the plot. The humans of Gondor avoid religion because they are afraid to repeat their early error of worshipping Sauron.

Humans and hobbits may not know Ilúvatar, God of Middle-earth; but in Tolkien's view, Middle-earth is very much his.

See also:
Galadriel
Gandalf

HOW DO YOU PLAY THE "RIDDLE-GAME"?

A HERO MUST be clever. In Chapter Five of *The Hobbit* (recounted in the prologue to *LOTR*), Bilbo is forced to match wits with Gollum. The contest is a duel of riddles. At stake is Bilbo's life.

When Tolkien first wrote that chapter, he was just having fun with a game that he encountered when studying Old English. The same ancient books that contain serious literature, like the poems Tolkien studied and taught at university, include many riddles. The scholars who wrote those old books considered riddle-making to be a real test of skill. And they weren't the first to think so. Riddles appear in serious books all the way back to the earliest literature, and all over

the world. For instance, riddles are found in the earliest Hindu text, the Rig-Veda, dating back to well before 1000 B.C. (What father has 730 children? A year, because it has 365 days and 365 nights.)

Riddle contests are also an old idea. In a legend of ancient Greece, a monster known as the Sphinx will not let travelers pass a certain spot unless they can answer a riddle that is still famous today:

What animal goes on four feet in the morning,
Two at noon,
And three in the evening?

The Great Sphinx in Giza is one of hundreds of sphinx statues built by ancient Egyptians, who first imagined the monster.

After eating many travelers who didn't know the answer, the Sphinx was beaten by the hero Oedipus, who guessed it: "Man creeps on hands and knees in childhood, walks upright in adulthood, and in old age uses a cane." (J. K. Rowling's hero Harry Potter meets a Sphinx who asks the same riddle. Harry also answers correctly.)

Like the riddle of the Sphinx, many old riddles are about common things. Anglo-Saxon riddles, for instance, mention swords, bows, shields, armor, keys, and animals. One reads:

> *I saw four fine creatures*
> *traveling in company; their tracks were dark,*
> *their trail very black. The bird that floats*
> *in the air swoops less swiftly than their leader;*
> *he dived beneath the wave. Drudgery was it*
> *for the fellow who taught all four*
> *   of them their ways*
> *on their ceaseless visits to the vessel of gold.*

Many readers note that Bilbo's final question to Gollum isn't even a riddle. He simply asks what he has in his pocket. That's like Rumpelstiltskin asking the miller's daughter to guess his name. It's not very fair. Tolkien says Bilbo was just nervous.

The answer: handwriting. Fingers hold the pen, which is dipped "beneath the wave" of ink in the inkwell. The "tracks" left behind are the words.

More than just fun, riddles can be a test of

your imagination. How many ways can you find to describe ordinary objects? Consider this one:

Millions of black ants:
The army marches forward in thousands
*   of platoons;*
In six brigades;
In three divisions;
All towards the One.

Millions of letters, forming thousands of words, arranged in six sections, and published in three volumes, tell the story of the One Ring: *The Lord of the Rings.*
Your turn.

See also:
Beowulf

DID OTHER RINGS INSPIRE TOLKIEN?

TRY TO IMAGINE *LOTR* without the One Ring. Impossible? Yet that's how the story began.

As soon as *The Hobbit* appeared, Tolkien's publisher and readers wanted another story like it. But Tolkien had other thoughts. He wanted his next book to be the legends about Middle-earth's creation, which he had been writing over the previous decades. Here is what Middle-earth is *really* about, Tolkien explained: not just dragons and treasure, but powerful forces and big ideas. His publisher wasn't interested. Those legends explained the background of Bilbo's world, but they didn't have the excitement of an adventure story.

Tolkien was disappointed, but he saw their point. So he started to write another story just

In the 1960s, the Beatles wanted to star in a film of *LOTR*. Frodo would have been played by Paul McCartney, Sam Gamgee by Ringo Starr, Gandalf by George Harrison, and Gollum by John Lennon. Imagine!

like the one in *The Hobbit.* As mentioned earlier, his idea was that Bilbo Baggins has spent
all the treasure won during the first adventure. Needing more, he goes on another
treasure hunt.

But as Tolkien tried to satisfy his readers,
he disappointed himself. He just wasn't interested in writing the same story again. And
wealth wasn't a good goal for his hero. He
hadn't created a whole imaginary world just to
write about money.

The serious ideas from the early legends
were still on his mind. He wondered how the
new story might grow to include them. He
wanted the story to be on a grander scale, and
darker. He wanted it to be about fighting
great evil. Still, he knew that he had to link
the new story to the old to please his publishers and readers. Suddenly, he had an idea.

In *The Hobbit,* Bilbo found a ring in Gollum's cave. Though it had the power to make
the wearer disappear, it didn't play a big part
in the story. But that didn't matter to Tolkien.
He knew magic rings are often very important
in legend, and very powerful. They appear in
legends from all over the world. As previously
discussed, Gollum's ring in *The Hobbit* comes
from a Norse legend about a dwarf called
Andvari, who has a magic ring stolen from

The "ring" in *The Hobbit* doesn't have a capital R, because its importance isn't known to the characters until Gandalf works out it is the One Ring. Of course, Tolkien himself didn't know its importance until he worked out the story of *LOTR*.

him. He puts a curse on anyone who tries to keep it. Awful things happen as a result. So, might there be a curse on Bilbo's ring? Tolkien jotted down a note to himself: "Make *return of ring* a motive" (*Tolkien* by H. Carpenter, 186).

At that moment, the whole story had a new direction: instead of looking for more treasure, Bilbo needed to get rid of the old treasure he had won. And the slightly magical "ring" of *The Hobbit* was now the evil "One Ring." From there, many pieces that Tolkien had already created fell into place.

Tolkien began to wonder about the Ring as if it were a character. What powers does it have? How does it come to have them? He came to an interesting conclusion: it might give great power, but at a great price. And merely possessing it is dangerous. As he said: "it exacts its penalty. You must either lose it, or *yourself*" (*Tolkien* by H. Carpenter, 186).

The Ring now had evil *within* it. That also fits with legend, as Tolkien knew. Many rings in literature contain a spirit or soul. A story from Jewish lore, for example, says the archangel Michael gave King Solomon a magic ring to imprison the souls of evil genies. Solomon made the genies build a large temple, then cast them into the Red Sea.

Some readers notice *LOTR* is similar to a German opera, *The Ring of the Nibelungs*. That's because the opera's composer, Richard Wagner, used many of the legends Tolkien later used, like the story of Andvari. Tolkien did not copy Wagner. They use the legends very differently.

From legends like this, Tolkien understood how to explain why the Ring was so evil: it would contain evil from a great enemy. With that flash of insight, the final plot of *LOTR* became clear: because the Ring contained some of the enemy's strength, the enemy could be defeated if the Ring were destroyed.

THE RING LORD

And who was this nameless enemy? Tolkien didn't have to think about that very long. The question was answered by another piece of *The Hobbit* he had been trying to put in the new book—a character described as "an enemy quite beyond the powers of all the dwarves put together" (*The Hobbit* by J.R.R. Tolkien, 37). Though Tolkien had mentioned the character only briefly and vaguely in *The Hobbit*, the combination of mystery and power had captured the interest of readers. They had asked for more about him. Without knowing it, they had pointed Tolkien in the right direction.

In *The Hobbit*, the character is called the Necromancer. Tolkien plucked the name from Norse mythology. Meaning "enchanter" or "wizard," it is a nickname often given to the most powerful Norse god, Odin. (It refers to the sorcerer's skill of speaking with the dead

In German, Odin's name becomes "Woden," and is the source of "Wednesday," meaning "Woden's day."

Odin is often pictured with his animal companions: two ravens, Hugin (thought) and Munin (memory), and his wolves, Geri and Freki.

to gain knowledge. *Necro* means "corpse" in ancient Greek.) Odin gets the nickname because, like the character in *The Hobbit*, he often likes to keep his identity a secret. He doesn't want people to know he is a god. This makes his great powers seem like just a wizard's magic.

Odin is a complicated figure. He is both good and evil. Because he can be generous, some readers say they see his personality in

Gandalf. That's partly true. But there is a much darker side to Odin's character. Just as he gives, he takes. He does not hesitate to kill if it suits his plans. He decides when his favorite heroes must die. He obeys no law but his own. No one can trust him completely. The Necromancer of *The Hobbit* was inspired by these dark qualities of Odin.

As it happened, there were links between Odin's role in legend and the Necromancer's new role in *LOTR*. For one, Odin plays a part in the legend of the dwarf Andvari. He is the one who arranges the theft of the dwarf's ring. As well, Odin has his own powerful ring—one of the most powerful in any mythology. It is called Draupnir ("Dropper"). It produces eight new golden rings every nine days, giving Odin endless wealth and power. With the rings from Draupnir, Odin buys loyalty and controls kings, just as Sauron would use the Rings of Power to tempt the leaders of the Elves, Dwarves, and humans.

Tolkien had finally found a way to fit his serious ideas into the new adventure, while keeping a link with *The Hobbit*. Following the patterns in legend, he now had a Lord and a Ring. The story was up and running.

See also:

Baggins, Bilbo

Gandalf

Gollum

Sauron

WHY DO THE ELVES MAKE THE RINGS?

YOU MIGHT FIND it hard to believe, but Elves aren't always good. In fact, when they're bad, the results can be disastrous.

The examples of Galadriel, Legolas, and Arwen seem admirable. Galadriel is kind and generous when the Fellowship visits Loth-lórien. Legolas contributes fearlessly to the cause of the Fellowship, and befriends Gimli the Dwarf despite the ancient anger between their two races.

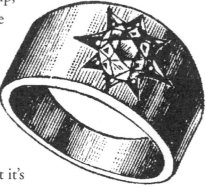

Yet in some ways, Elves have the same goal as Sauron: to control the world. That's quite an accusation, but it's what Tolkien believed.

REVENGE OF THE NERDS

The problem is that Elves like to tinker. One line of Elves in particular, the Noldorin ("knowledgeable"), is especially eager to understand how things work. This puts them, Tolkien says, "always on the side of 'science and technology' " (*The Letters of J.R.R. Tolkien* edited by H. Carpenter with C. Tolkien, 190). He didn't consider that a good thing. It's the sort of knowledge that interests Sauron and the other villains of Middle-earth. Saruman, for instance, is even described like a machine: he "has a mind of metal and wheels, and he does not care for growing things, except as far as they serve him for the moment" (*The Lord of the Rings* by J.R.R. Tolkien, 462). Meanwhile good characters, like hobbits, distrust machines.

Legolas the Elf is the only member of the Fellowship to prefer a bow and arrow. This may go back to ancient European legends of elves who shoot arrows from the sky. The legends arose from stories of old gods who threw thunderbolts.

THE BEST-LAID PLANS . . .

The Elves don't intend to do bad things, as Sauron and Saruman do. Yet bad things often happen because of good Elves. The Elves never imagined the Rings would one day be used for evil. Although each of the three Rings worn by Elves have positive qualities (for example, healing), they also allowed Sauron to make the Ruling Ring, with the power to undo all of that good. And even though the Elves didn't mean to help Sauron, Tolkien doesn't let them off the hook by blaming Sauron alone. He compared them to scientists in our world whose work might harm the environment or be used for weapons. He believed the Elves should have known better than to make the Rings of Power in the first place.

CLOCKWATCHERS

The creation of Rings reveals another flaw in the Elves' character, according to Tolkien. Living forever, he says, the Elves see many things pass away, and want to preserve a "fresh and fair" moment (*The Letters of J.R.R. Tolkien* edited by H. Carpenter with C. Tolkien, 236). They also like being the most advanced creatures on Earth, and don't want that to change, even though it's not fair to the others.

You might say Elves want to use the Rings to stop time. As Tolkien says, "the chief power (of all the rings alike) was the prevention or slowing of decay . . . the preservation of what is desired or loved" (*The Letters of J.R.R. Tolkien* edited by H. Carpenter with C. Tolkien, 152). You can see that power in the way the One Ring makes Bilbo's life longer

See also:

Elves

than usual for a hobbit, and keeps Gollum alive for hundreds of years. But the Elves' desire sets them against the plan of God: they are trying to take control of the world God has created. To a lesser degree, that's just what Sauron wants.

WHY MIGHT SAURON APPEAR AS A SINGLE EYE?

Sauron

ALTHOUGH THERE ARE a few references in *LOTR* to Sauron having a body (less the finger that was cut off when the Ring was taken from him), he generally appears in the frightening form of one all-seeing eye. Frodo sees the eye in the Mirror of Galadriel, and it scares him so much he can't move or speak. Orcs at the Dark Tower use a red eye as their mark, and refer to Sauron as the Great Eye.

One-eyed
monsters, such as
the Cyclops
encountered by
Hercules in the
Odyssey, are also
common in
legend. But these
monsters are not
to be confused
with gods such as
Ra or Odin.

I SPY, WITH MY LITTLE EYE . . .

Legends are full of one-eyed gods and demons. They are usually later versions of the sun gods of early history, such as the Egyptian god Ra. Sun gods (and moon gods) appear in nearly every early culture, from Mesopotamia (Iraq) to the Americas.

Often these one-eyed gods are able to see all. You can't keep a secret from them, in the same way that you can't escape the sun's glare. Gollum avoids the sun and the moon, because they remind him of Sauron's eye.

Even the later versions of sun gods often keep their original powers. In Celtic legend,

Hieroglyphs show
an offering to the
sun god Ra.

for example, the god Balar had a single fiery eye that could destroy whole armies at a time. (Tolkien uses his name for Bay of Balar and the Isle of Balar.)

AN EYE FOR AN EYE?

A particular one-eyed god of legend, who was originally a sun god, played an important role in shaping Sauron's character. As mentioned earlier, Odin, the chief god of Norse mythology, was an important inspiration for Tolkien when he first created Sauron. He was an early source for the Necromancer in *The Hobbit*, who eventually grew into the Dark Lord of *LOTR*.

Odin often wears a wide-brimmed hat to cover his missing eye, so people will not know he is a god.

Of all the many stories about Odin, the story of how he loses one eye may be the most important, because it reveals the source of his power. Always restless and searching for new wisdom and experience, Odin decides to drink from a special well that contains the world's knowledge. But that well, located at the root of the great tree that holds up the world, is guarded by the giant Mimir, who says he will give Odin only a taste—just one hornful of water. And even for that much, Odin must make a great sacrifice: he must give up one of his eyes. Odin thinks about it, then agrees. He gives it up, drinks from the well, then, just as he imagined, gains the wisdom that helps make him the greatest of the Norse gods. Afterwards he often appears as an old man with a single, blazing eye.

Odin asks Mimir for a drink from the well of knowledge.

WHAT'S THE WORST THING ABOUT SAURON?

LOOKING AT HOW Sauron treats Middle-earth, it is easy to think he simply enjoys bossing people around, or destroying what Ilúvatar, the God of Middle-earth, has created. But these aren't the worst things about him, in Tolkien's view. They are just signs of something worse.

THE DEADLIEST SIN OF ALL

Sauron thinks he's special because he has a broader collection of talents than the other spirits created by Ilúvatar. While most of them have only one or two parts of Ilúvatar's character in their personality, Sauron has a little bit of every part. He's proud of that, which is a mistake. He seems to forget that all those talents are gifts from Ilúvatar, whose own are greater still. Because of his pride, he goes too far. He tries to play God.

Tolkien says the most important message of *LOTR* is "about God, and His sole right to divine honor" (*The Letters of J.R.R. Tolkien* edited by H. Carpenter with C. Tolkien, 243). Tolkien says God deserves that honor because only He can create. Sauron wants to share that honor.

So Sauron is not evil simply because he destroys. Rather, he is evil because he tries to create. In fact, Sauron doesn't even need to destroy to be satisfied. He just wants to reign as a Creator within his world, and to be worshipped as one.

PRIDE GOETH BEFORE A FALL

It's often said that Sauron resembles the Biblical figure Satan. (The story of Satan, briefly, is that he is a fallen angel. He presumes to challenge God, and tricks Adam and

Eve into disobeying God's will. As a result, they are exiled from Paradise.) Critic Randel Helms declares the stories of Sauron and Satan align "point by point." A few thousand years before *LOTR* begins, Sauron tricks a group of humans into defying the angelic spirits. As a result, the beautiful island home of the humans is destroyed. The few humans who survive are driven to Middle-earth, just as Adam and Eve are driven from Eden.

The comparison is fair. Yet even when Tolkien considered Sauron's worst acts, he found a way to overcome his disgust. He had compassion for Sauron, just as he had compassion for Gollum. In Tolkien's world, even the

Adam and Eve are escorted from Eden after falling for Satan's tricks and defying God—just as the Númenóreans are driven from their island paradise after falling for Sauron's lies.

worst acts can be forgiven. For instance, the Valar who first shapes the Dwarves is also trying to be a Creator, but because he repents that sin Ilúvatar rewards him by giving life to the Dwarves.

Tolkien never forgot the lesson he was taught about Satan: Satan was not always evil, nor was he completely evil. Likewise, Sauron could not be pure evil. Tolkien even declares that philosophy outright in *LOTR*: "Nothing is evil in the beginning," Elrond Halfelven tells the Fellowship. "Even Sauron was not so" (*The Lord of the Rings* by J.R.R. Tolkien, 261).

See also:

Dwarves

Gondor

Religion

Silmarillion, The

WHO WAS TOLKIEN'S FIRST DARK LORD?

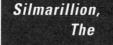

Silmarillion,
The

MANY WRITERS DRAW from old mythology or literature, but Tolkien went even further. He wrote his own ancient legends about Middle-earth's creation, then borrowed heavily from them when writing *LOTR*.

For more than two decades after *LOTR* first appeared, fans waited eagerly to read those legends of the First Age. When, at last, *The Silmarillion* was published, a few years after Tolkien's death, readers were amazed at what Tolkien had imagined and how he had connected it to *LOTR*. A lot of important facts about Middle-earth's Third Age suddenly fell into place. Most interesting were the tales of a Dark Lord even more powerful and more evil than Sauron.

Just as *LOTR* is supposedly a translation of the diaries of Bilbo and others, Tolkien says *The Silmarillion* comes from Elven books that Bilbo found.

PARALLEL LIVES

The parallels between *The Silmarillion* and *LOTR* are fascinating and revealing, starting with the objects at the center of each story. *The Silmarillion* gets its name from the Silmarils, three beautiful jewels. Like the Rings of Powers in *LOTR*, the Silmarils are made by Elves, and for the same reason: they want to preserve something beautiful. In *LOTR*, they wish to preserve certain aspects of Middle-earth; in *The Silmarillion*, they want to capture the light of the Two Trees of Valinor, magnificent creations that shine and dim, in turn, on a twelve-hour cycle. In another parallel, both the Rings of Power and the Silmarils have special qualities because they contain powerful forces. The One Ring that Tolkien created for *LOTR* is the mirror-image of the Silmarils: it contains the essence of the Dark Lord—a neat storytelling twist on the jewels, which hold light.

Tolkien's use of his own legends in *LOTR* includes characters copied from originals in *The Silmarillion*, and again the First Age reveals much about the Third Age. Galadriel's mother role in *LOTR* is close to the role played by Varda, one of the angelic powers that shape Middle-earth, in *The Silmarillion*. The obstacles

Tolkien had hoped to publish his legends after *The Hobbit,* but his editors felt a collection of legends would be too different from the single adventure that readers had enjoyed in the first book. And perhaps more important, there weren't any hobbits in the stories. So Tolkien set to work on the story that became *LOTR.*

faced by Aragorn and Arwen in *LOTR* are like those that stand in the way of Beren and Lúthien in *The Silmarillion*. In fact, Arwen is said to look exactly like Lúthien, as if she is the same character. Even the giant spider Shelob in *LOTR* has a counterpart in *The Silmarillion*: the evil Ungoliant.

In each of these cases, the character from *The Silmarillion* is grander and more powerful than the *LOTR* version. That makes sense: *The Silmarillion* is about the great forces that make and shape the whole universe, not just Middle-earth. It begins even before the universe exists, then tells of its creation, step by step.

The character in *The Silmarillion* who parallels Sauron's role in *LOTR* shows the same extra strength—and extra evil. He is Melkor, the first Dark Lord, also known as the Great Enemy. (Melkor is known among the Elves as "Morgoth," a name given to him by the Elf who created the Silmarils. It means "Dark Enemy.") Like the Valar who shape Middle-earth, Melkor is an angelic spirit. In

Sixty years
passed between
Tolkien's start of
The Silmarillion in
1917 and its first
publication.
Tolkien was too
busy after the
success of *LOTR*
to finish it to his
satisfaction. After
his death the
work was done by
his son
Christopher, with
the help of Guy
Gavriel Kay, who
has since become
a famous author
himself.

fact, he is the most powerful spirit of all.
While the others were each created by the
God of Tolkien's world, Ilúvatar, from a single part of his own personality, Melkor has
some of each part. These extra gifts lead him
to think he's as good as Ilúvatar. That's where
the trouble begins. Soon he's trying to act
like a god.

Of the many evils acts Melkor commits,
among the worst comes from his hunger for
the Silmarils, which is like Sauron's desire for
the Ring in *LOTR*. Melkor, jealous of the
light created by the Two Trees of Valinor, and

of the Silmarils, destroys the trees and steals the jewels. And just like the War of the Ring caused by Sauron in *LOTR*, Melkor's crime in *The Silmarillion* leads to war: in the War of the Great Jewels, Melkor and the Elves struggle for possession of the powerful objects.

Rather than just using Melkor for inspiration when creating Sauron, Tolkien made the parallels between the two characters into part of the story: Sauron is Melkor's assistant. Melkor gives Sauron some of the extra powers given him by Ilúvatar. That's why it's so hard for other characters in *LOTR*, like Gandalf, to oppose Sauron directly.

In 1992, when Tolkien would have been 100 years old, two clubs of serious Tolkien readers (the Tolkien Society and the Mythopoeic Society) planted a pair of trees as a memorial in a park at Oxford.

WHERE'S MELKOR?

Melkor's story ends in *The Silmarillion* when he is cast out of the universe by Ilúvatar, who has had enough of his troublemaking. That's a clever trick on Ilúvatar's part, but it raises a question. Why doesn't he do the same with Sauron?

The answer lies in Tolkien's ideas about good and evil. Melkor may be evil, but he was originally created by God, so he is a natural part of the universe. The end of Melkor's story can't mean the end of evil on Earth. Good and evil are always present, Tolkien believed, and always will be. That's why Ilúvatar lets Sauron have a place in the world.

That's also why Tolkien considered it natural to draw on the legends of *The Silmarillion*, and put so many parallels in *LOTR*: history repeats itself. The battle between good and evil never ends.

See also:

Languages

Religion

Rings

Sauron

WHY IS FRODO'S "PHIAL OF GALADRIEL" SO POWERFUL?

Silmarillion, The

LIKE MOST HEROES, Frodo is given amulets—magical tools to help him on his journey. Some have obvious uses. He will need the sword Sting, given to him by Bilbo, if he meets enemies. He'll also be protected by the vest made of mithril, a strong and rare metal. However, the importance of a gift from Galadriel—a small phial containing shining water from her magical fountain—is not obvious at first. Yet it may be the most powerful of all. Its fascinating origin is a poem that obsessed Tolkien for more than two decades, until he placed the phial in Frodo's hands. By then, the poem had grown into an important part of Middle-earth's history.

"STAR LIGHT, STAR BRIGHT . . ."

As Galadriel explains to Frodo, the water in the phial has caught the light of a special star. That star is actually one of the Silmarils, the light-capturing jewels made by Elves. It is linked to the story of a man named Eärendil, which Bilbo tells the night before the Council of Elrond meets to decide on a plan for the Ring. In short, it goes like this: Eärendil makes a dangerous sea journey to ask the ruling powers of Middle-earth, the Valar, to end a long war. The light of the Silmaril helps him find the way. The Valar, impressed with his faith and bravery, grant his wish, then immortalize him by placing him in the sky with the Silmaril as a sign of hope to those below.

Like the light of Eärendil in the sky, Galadriel's phial bestows hope and courage. When things get tough for Frodo and Sam— such as when they meet a hungry, many-eyed monster in the dark—it is a precious gift.

The legend behind the phial comes from the first story Tolkien wrote about Middle-earth, more than twenty years before he wrote *LOTR*. The idea came suddenly, as he read two lines from a poem written in Old English:

Eala Earendel engla beorhtast
Ofer middangeard monnum sended

In modern English they say:

Hail Earendel, brightest of angels
Above middle-earth sent unto men.

"I felt a curious thrill," Tolkien later said,
"as if something had stirred in me, half awak-
ened from sleep. There was something very
remote and strange and beautiful behind
these words, something far beyond ancient
English" (*Tolkien* by H. Carpenter, 64).

TOLKIEN'S HERALD

In the poem, the star announces the birth of
Jesus Christ. But Tolkien believed the lines
came from some earlier legend, first told long
before people heard of Jesus. He was determined to use his knowledge of word history
to discover that "strange and beautiful" meaning. Knowing "Earendel" is made from Old
English words meaning "star" and "dawn," he
guessed it came from a legend about a bright
star that announces the "birth" of the dawn
each day, by appearing in the sky before the
sun. (That "star," as Tolkien knew, is actually
the planet Venus.)

In time, Tolkien was inspired by those two
lines to write a poem of his own about the
star, and of a sailor whose ship flies through

The poem that
inspired Tolkien,
entitled *Crist* [as
in "Christ"], was
probably written
in the ninth
century. Little is
known about the
Anglo-Saxon
author, Cynewulf.

the heavens. As biographer Humphrey Carpenter says, this marked "the beginning of Tolkien's own mythology" (*Tolkien* by H. Carpenter, 71).

Though Tolkien reworked his legend many times before linking it to Frodo's quest, he never forgot the source. The words that automatically come to Frodo when he uses the phial—*"Aiya Eärendil Elenion Ancalima!"*—are the words in Tolkien's invented Elvish language for the phrase Tolkien had read decades before: "Hail Earendel, brightest of angels." What had been a guiding star for Tolkien as a writer became the guiding star of Middle-earth.

See also:

Galadriel

Tolkien

Undying Lands

WHICH MONSTER ATTACKED TOLKIEN?

ONE OF THE most dangerous creatures in *LOTR* is the giant spider, Shelob. More gruesome than an Orc, stronger than a dragon, she waits in her lair with a special sort of evil intent. Unlike Sauron, who wants to dominate hobbits, Elves, Dwarves, and humans, Shelob simply wants to eat them. No discussion. No great moral battle. Just dinner.

Shelob might seem familiar if you've read *The Hobbit*. In that story, Bilbo Baggins meets a whole gang of Dwarf-eating spiders. And in an early legend that became part of *The Silmarillion*, Tolkien created another evil giant spider, Ungoliant.

Obviously, he was stuck on the idea. And he had plenty of company. Repulsive, man-eating spiders are nothing new in legend and literature. They go back long before any written tradition and appear all over the world. The Lakota tribe of Native Americans tells many stories of one called Unktomi. More recently, Harry Potter creator J. K. Rowling invented Aragog, Mosag, and their children, who also find humans delicious. No doubt Tolkien knew many spider legends from his

studies. One author he enjoyed as a child, Lord Dunsany, wrote of a large, talking spider, with eyes "in which there was much sin," who spun his web for "the honor of Satan."

Yet according to biographer Humphrey Carpenter, Tolkien met the source of Shelob before he could read. While still an infant in South Africa, just as he was learning to walk, he encountered a tarantula in his family's garden. As many people know, tarantulas are no ordinary spiders: they can be almost as large as an adult's hand, and are usually hairy. They live in holes they dig underground. They bite with two huge fangs, pumping a poison into their prey that can liquefy the guts of insects and smaller animals.

And, though tarantulas don't commonly bite people, they'll do so if accidentally disturbed or if touched by, say, a curious infant. That's just what Tolkien's spider did. Tolkien "ran in terror across the garden until the nurse picked him up and sucked out the poison," Carpenter says. "When he grew up he could remember a hot day and running in fear through long, dead grass" (*Tolkien* by H. Carpenter, 13).

Tolkien didn't have a visual memory of the tarantula itself, and never developed a special

Tolkien was born in South Africa in 1892, a few years after his parents moved there from England.

In 1896, when Tolkien was visiting England with his mother and brother, his father passed away suddenly. The family did not return to South Africa.

See also:

Gollum

Orcs

fear of spiders—he sometimes caught small ones in his home in Oxford to release them outside. But in his imagination, the day he was bitten was the day Shelob was born.

WHY DO THE BEST SWORDS BREAK?

GOOD THINGS TAKE time. In legend, swords often require years of forging, usually by elf or dwarf smiths, whose powers are beyond those of mere humans. According to one legend, it took three years to forge a sword for King Charlemagne.

Yet the swords of heroes often break at the worst possible moment. In Middle-earth, one broken sword is mentioned again and again. It is the great sword Narsil, used to cut the Ring from Sauron's hand thousands of years before *LOTR* begins. Despite being shaped by the most gifted smith of the Dwarves, it snaps in two just when it is needed most: when Elendil, the first High King of Arnor and Gondor, is trying to finish off Sauron.

Is the loss of Narsil an accident? Not at all. In stories like *LOTR*, how heroes win or lose swords is not a matter of luck.

THE SWORD IN THE . . . TREE?

Great swords must be earned or given as a gift. The new owner should show he or she is worthy above all others. In the King Arthur legends, the wizard Merlin uses magic to stick a sword into a stone so that only the true king, young Arthur, can remove it. In some Arthur legends, a second sword is given to the king by the mysterious Lady of the Lake.

The idea for Arthur's sword in the stone was borrowed from the Icelandic legend

King Arthur, shown here with Merlin, is offered a sword by the mysterious Lady of the Lake.

Volsunga, which recounts how the great hero Sigmund wins his weapon:

> King Volsung built a noble hall with a big oak tree inside, called the Branstock; the limbs of the tree blossomed far out over the roof of the hall. One evening an unknown man came into the hall, barefoot, wearing a dirty cloak. He had a sword in his hand as he went up to the Branstock, and a slouched hat upon his head. Huge he was, and old, and one-eyed. He stuck the sword into the tree, sinking it to the hilt. Then he spoke:
>
> "Who can draw this sword from this tree, shall have it as a gift from me, and shall find that there is better sword than this." Then the old man left the hall, and none knew where he went.
>
> The men stood up. None wanted to be the last to lay hand to the sword, for they believed that the first to touch it would have it. All the noblest went first, then the others; but none could pull it out, however hard they tugged at it. Now up comes Sigmund, King Volsung's son. He sets hand to the sword, and pulls it from the tree as if it lay loose. None had seen such a sword before. Siggeir tried to buy

Great swords never merely cut. Like Sting, which glows when Orcs are near, they may warn of danger; or, like Excalibur, they may light the darkness. Some are enchanted, and protect their heroes from danger. In modern fiction, Terry Pratchett writes of a sword that speaks in *The Color of Magic*.

it from him at thrice its weight of gold, but Sigmund said: "Thou might have taken the sword, if it had been thy lot to bear it; but now, since it has fallen into my hand, never shalt thou have it."

Like Frodo's Sting and Aragorn's Andúril, most swords of great heroes in history and legend have names: Arthur has Excalibur; Charlemagne has Joyeuse; Roland has Durandal; El Cid has Tizona and Colada— there are dozens of examples.

In *LOTR*, Frodo receives his sword Sting in just this way. Bilbo plunges Sting into a beam rather than handing it to Frodo directly. Frodo then removes it from the beam.

The reverse of this rule about earning a sword also holds true: to gain a sword dishonorably often leads to no good. Sometimes such a sword is found to be cursed. For instance, it might seem good at first, because it always kills one's enemy, but then the hero learns it can't be prevented from killing, and tragedy follows. In the Finnish epic *Kalevala*, one of Tolkien's influences, the villain Kullervo gains his sword by murder, an act of dishonor that is corrected when the sword takes Kullervo's life. Tolkien followed that story closely in his tale of Túrin Turambar in *The Silmarillion*.

BROKEN SWORDS

How a hero loses a sword is also a serious matter. A good example is Tolkien's story of the human king Elendil, whose sword Narsil is broken in a battle with Sauron three thousand years before the action of *LOTR*. The idea of a broken sword comes from the *Volsunga* story described earlier: after Sigmund removes the sword from the tree, he has many great adventures. The god Odin, who happens to be the mysterious one-eyed stranger who put the sword in the tree in the first place, decides it is time for Sigmund to die and join the gods. He appears again, this time on a battlefield,

> clad in a blue cloak, and with a slouched hat on his head, one-eyed he was, and nothing but a staff in his hand. He came against Sigmund the King, and raised up his staff, and as Sigmund smote fiercely the sword struck the staff and broke in half. Sigmund's good luck had left him.

Sigmund dies that day, but his widow keeps the broken sword. When their son Sigurd is grown, she gives him the pieces. He eventually has them mended, and becomes a great dragon-slaying hero himself.

In this legend, as in many others, the best swords break so that no one else can wield them until a worthy successor appears. The restored sword is both the signal and the means by which a rightful dynasty is restored.

In Sir Thomas Malory's *Le Morte d'Arthur*, Sir Galahad and other knights find a sword on a strange ship. They learn the sword goes back to the time of King Solomon, and the ship has carried it through the ages to find the rightful owner. Galahad proves worthy of this sword.

That theme is important to *LOTR*. Elendil's son Isildur is able to use the broken sword to cut the Ring from Sauron's hand, but he cannot repair the sword. Apparently something about him is unworthy—a fact confirmed when he is corrupted by the Ring. However, the sword is repaired (and renamed Andúril) for Aragorn, because he is the rightful heir of Gondor and has the willpower to refuse the Ring. As Tolkien puts it several times, "Renewed shall be the blade that was broken/ The crownless again shall be king" (*The Lord of the Rings* by J.R.R. Tolkien, 167).

Sigurd (shown here with Brunhild, the warrior queen of Iceland) holds the sword he inherited from his father. Broken in his father's final battle, it was reforged when he was ready to become a great hero.

WHY DID TOLKIEN WRITE ABOUT A "FELLOWSHIP"?

Tolkien, J.R.R.

ELROND HALFELVEN KNOWS just what it takes to challenge the nine Black Riders who hunt the Ring: a band of nine brothers in arms, the Fellowship of the Ring.

Imagining a fellowship was natural for Tolkien, who had a passion for starting clubs in real life. For instance, there was the Viking Club, formed with a fellow Anglo-Saxon scholar when both were teaching at Leeds University. It included undergraduates and "met to drink large quantities of beer, read sagas, and sing comic songs" written by Tolkien and his friend (*Tolkien* by H. Carpenter, 105). When he moved to Oxford University, he founded another Norse literature club (with less drinking and more reading) called the Coalbiters, for fellow lecturers. Most famously, he was a member of the Inklings. This group lasted for about twenty years and included C. S. Lewis, who was eventually converted to Christianity by Tolkien and went on to write *The Lion, the Witch and the Wardrobe* and the other Narnia books. But the most important club for Tolkien may have been his first.

TEA AND SYMPATHY

In 1911, when Tolkien was nineteen years old, he was a student at King Edward's School in Birmingham. As you might expect, he spent a lot of time in the school library. And it was a tradition at the school that a few boys in the senior class would be given the title "Librarian." Naturally, Tolkien was one of them.

He and the other boys joined in an informal fellowship. They called themselves the "Tea Club," and then, because they sometimes had tea at Barrow's Stores, the "Barrovian Society." Soon it became "T.C.B.S." for short. The members, all bright and knowledgeable, shared their individual enthusiasms with

each other. "Tolkien's contribution," says biographer Humphrey Carpenter, "reflected the wide range of reading he had already encompassed. He delighted his friends with recitations from *Beowulf, Pearl* [another Anglo-Saxon poem], and *Sir Gawain and the Green Knight,* and recounted horrific episodes from the Norse *Völsungasaga"* (*Tolkien* by H. Carpenter, 46). He also told them of his desire to write an epic work of mythology, and they encouraged him.

There's no telling how long the T.C.B.S. would have lasted if World War I hadn't intruded. In 1916, Tolkien was shipped along with hundreds of thousands of British troops to France. Two of his friends from the T.C.B.S., Geoffrey Bache Smith and Rob Gilson, were also there, in different battalions. (The last member was in the navy.) In the midst of the terrible fighting—an astonishing number of men were killed or wounded— Tolkien and his friends sent each other messages whenever possible. Then a note came with awful news: Rob Gilson had been killed.

Tolkien was devastated. The other T.C.B.S friend in France, G. B. Smith, tried to console him. "Death can make us loathsome and help-

Tolkien's son Christopher was named for T.C.B.S companion Christopher Wiseman, whose friendship with Tolkien lasted to the end of Tolkien's life.

less as individuals," Smith wrote to Tolkien, "but it cannot put an end to the immortal four!" (*Tolkien* by H. Carpenter, 86). Not long afterwards, Smith was also dead.

The Fellowship had disappeared. There was now only Tolkien and one other T.C.B.S. companion left—the friend serving in the navy, Christopher Wiseman. Wiseman sent a note to Tolkien, who was in England, recovering from an illness picked up in the trenches. "You ought to start the epic," Wiseman wrote (*Tolkien* by H. Carpenter, 90). Tolkien agreed, spurred on by strong feelings. Shortly before being killed, G. B. Smith had written him: "[I]f I am scuppered tonight . . . there will be left a member of the great T.C.B.S. to voice what I dreamed and what we agreed upon" (*Tolkien* by H. Carpenter, 86). Soon Tolkien was writing the first legends that would eventually become Middle-earth's story, and which would lead, a few decades later, to another great fellowship.

See also:

Elves

Was G. B. Smith right to say the T.C.B.S. was immortal? It seems he was.

WHY ARE THERE SO MANY TOWERS?

Towers

POP QUIZ: WHICH are the towers mentioned in the title of *LOTR*'s second volume, *The Two Towers*? If you have a quick answer to that question you're ahead of Tolkien. For a long time he wasn't sure.

HIGH AND MIGHTY

Dark towers are a common feature of the literary landscape, with good reason. Rising high to defy nature, they signify power and wealth. They suggest a limitless view. They can be prisons. These ideas come from real life: towers, such as the Tower of London, were often the home of monarchs, making them the site of palace intrigue or even murder.

In Middle-earth you'll find more than half

By the time
volume titles
were being
decided for *LOTR*,
Tolkien's editor
at the firm of
Allen & Unwin
was Rayner
Unwin. Rayner
had been reading
portions of the
book since he
was a young boy.
His father, an
owner of the firm,
had first asked
him to read
Tolkien to help
decide whether
The Hobbit should
be published.
Rayner's
enthusiasm led
to his father's
decision.

a dozen. Some are filled with Orcs. Gandalf is imprisoned in another. One is home to the Black Riders. Sauron's eye stares out of yet another.

Tolkien was very aware of the emotions conjured up by this symbol. He refers to Dark Towers often: in the prologue to *LOTR*, he explains the peaceful nature of hobbits by saying, "They did not go in for towers"; later, Frodo is told Sauron's Dark Tower has risen again, and Gandalf scares Pippin by explaining that Sauron wants to torture him in the Dark Tower (*The Lord of the Rings* by J.R.R. Tolkien, 7, 43, 580). These are just a few of many examples.

WHICH ARE "THE TWO TOWERS"?

With all his talk about towers, you would think Tolkien might know which towers he had in mind for the title of the second volume of *LOTR*. After all, he did write the story. But he never intended the story to appear as three separate books. That was decided by his publisher, because of the cost of printing. The publisher also suggested "The Two Towers" as the title of the second book.

Tolkien agreed that it sounded nice, but it didn't really make sense. He could not say which two towers stood out as the two most important. For months he tried to decide which two towers should be the ones in the title, so he could make that clear in the story and show them on the book jacket. He wasn't even sure if the title was supposed to refer to two Dark Towers under Sauron's control, or one of Sauron's and one controlled by the forces fighting him. He went so far as to design different book jackets, showing the variations.

He finally decided it had to refer to two Dark Towers, Orthanc and Cirith Ungol. Even then, he wasn't completely sure. (The LOTR filmmakers changed this to Orthanc

and Barad-dûr, the dark towers of Saruman
and Sauron.)

In the end, it probably didn't matter. Just
the suggestion of towers brings to mind something ageless and haunting, as Tolkien must
have sensed when he created so many.

ARE THE UNDYING LANDS HEAVEN?

BECAUSE TOLKIEN WAS a devout Catholic, and
Christianity influenced his stories, you might
think all the important elements of
Christianity have a place in his
mythology. And what could be
more important than the promised
afterlife? But make no assumptions
about the Undying Lands. They have a
complex origin.

DON'T LET THE SUN GO DOWN ON ME
Although by the time of *LOTR* the Undying
Lands are hidden from the physical world
humans can see, they were once the continent
of Aman and the island of Eressëa, far to the
west of Middle-earth, across a vast ocean.
Aman is the home of the immortal angelic
spirits who shape the world, and of some

Elves. And though the humans cannot find the Undying Lands, they keep trying. They often tell stories about them.

Tolkien did not locate the Undying Lands in the western ocean by accident. He was following ancient traditions. In many cultures the setting sun was said to point the way to these special places. For instance, the ancient Greeks revered Elysium, the Islands of the Blessed, located past the edge of the ocean.

A few of these lands are places where only spirits may go after death. But many, such as the enchanted lands of Celtic legend, which influenced Tolkien, are places one goes *before* death. And the trip is usually made by boat. Two legendary Celtic races that influenced Tolkien's ideas of Elves—the Tuatha Dé Danaan and the Sidhe—were said to have left Ireland for "Tír na nÓg," an enchanted island to the west that closely resembles the Blessed Realm, where Valar and Elves live.

Even after Christian ideas of heaven were introduced to Britain, the old ideas of enchanted lands didn't fully disappear. They mixed with Christianity in stories called *imrama* ("voyages" in Gaelic). These combine an ocean journey with a search for Christian paradise. Tolkien himself wrote a poem entitled

Tolkien's poem "Imram" tells the story of St. Brendan the Navigator, who some people claim was the first European to sail the Atlantic and reach the Americas.

"Imram," which retells the story of a sixth-century Irish abbot who sails off to find paradise.

THE MISTS OF AVALON

It was Tolkien's idea that the legends we hear about these lands are faint echoes of the stories told by the humans of Middle-earth. And he even used a neat linguistic trick to connect *LOTR* to a particular Celtic legend about King Arthur, who is taken by boat to an enchanted land called "Avalon" after being fatally wounded. Tolkien arranged his High-elven language so one of the names for the Undying Lands is *Avallónë* ("near the home of

With the idea of afterworlds across the sea came the idea of placing the dead in boats, as is done for Boromir in *LOTR*. Below, King Arthur's half sister Elaine floats on a death barge.

the Valar"). He wanted us to think that the King Arthur legends, which take place long after *LOTR*, draw the name "Avalon" from the *real* story which he had set down.

And just as in the story of King Arthur, *Avallónë* is not heaven. It is an enchanted place where wounds are healed and time passes slowly. One lives among the great elves and fairies, as if one were living with the gods. It is not an end. It is a trip to a place where one can rest peacefully until death comes.

See also:

Elves

IS THE WAR
OF THE RING
BASED ON
WORLD WAR II?

BECAUSE *LOTR* WAS published in 1954, about a decade after the Second World War ended, many readers assumed Tolkien based his war in Middle-earth on the war in Europe. They thought they saw facts from real history repeated in the novel: the evil forces in both the war and the novel are lead by a detestable dictator; allies have to set aside petty differences to fight a common enemy; the One Ring seems all-powerful, like WWII's atomic bomb.

THE RING AND THE BOMB

Tolkien was annoyed by these assumptions. Too simple, he said. Too obvious. As he explained, he had imagined the plot before the war began. He created the Fellowship of the Ring long before the Allies joined forces in real life. The power of the Ring became the focus of the story eight years before the atomic bomb was invented. In fact, many of his ideas about war were actually formed during his service in the *First* World War, almost three decades before he wrote *LOTR*.

However, while *LOTR* doesn't follow the day-to-day facts of the Second World War, the war certainly did affect Tolkien's thinking. In several letters (some to his sons, who served in the armed forces), he connects ideas in the story to events of the day. For example, though he did not mean the Ring to be a symbol for the atomic bomb, when he learned of the bomb's existence he was angry with the scientists who made it. The day the news broke, he wrote a letter to one of them: "The news today about 'Atomic bombs' is so horrifying one is stunned. The utter folly of these lunatic physicists to consent to do such work for war-purposes: calmly plotting the destruction of the world!" (*The Letters of J.R.R. Tolkien* edited by H. Carpenter with C. Tolkien, 116). Later he says those physicists were like the Elves who make the Rings of Power. They loved science, but were blind to its consequences.

In one battle in *LOTR* an umbrella-shaped cloud appears. Some readers think this is a reference to the atomic bomb's famous mushroom cloud. But the phenomenon is not uncommon after explosions. Tolkien saw it on the battlefields of France during the First World War.

Although Tolkien did not predict the war as he plotted the novel in 1936, afterwards he recognized that the war marked "a dark age" to "rival that of Mordor and the Ring" (*The Letters of J.R.R. Tolkien* edited by H. Carpenter with C. Tolkien, 234). Or, as his friend and fellow author C. S. Lewis put it, "These things were not devised to reflect any particular situation in the real world. It was the other way around; real events began, horribly, to conform to the pattern he had freely invented" (*Tolkien* by H. Carpenter, 190).

WAS TOLKIEN A PACIFIST?

Just as some people are too quick to connect real history to the plot of *LOTR*, some jump to conclusions about Tolkien's view of war.

In the book, it's easy to find strong suggestions of pacifism—the idea that all fighting is wrong. (Pacifists believe one must never take up arms, even to battle evil. The word comes from the Latin *pax*, meaning "peace.") For instance, he says in the prologue, "At no time had Hobbits of any kind been warlike" (*The Lord of the Rings* by J.R.R. Tolkien, 5). And Boromir, the most warlike of the Fellowship, is the first to fall victim to the Ring's evil pull, because he is so eager to use it as a weapon. In letters, Tolkien explained that the most

The origin of Tom Bombadil is a doll that had been stuck in a toilet! The doll belonged to one of Tolkien's sons. After "rescuing" it, Tolkien championed Tom in a poem. That's where the character first meets Goldberry, a water-nymph— a pretty bad joke, considering what happened to the doll.

important symbol of pacifism is Tom Bombadil, the strange character who saves the hobbits from Old Man Willow. Tom doesn't take either side in the struggle over the Ring. (He's so removed from the struggle that he doesn't even become invisible when he puts on the Ring.)

But while Tolkien wanted to show that pacifism is a common point of view, he didn't hold that view himself. He wanted *LOTR* to show that one must sometimes set aside a peaceful ideal and face evil directly. As he explains in a letter, Tom Bombadil's survival depends on the Fellowship's quest.

You might say Tolkien was like Frodo: a reluctant warrior. He believed the flaws in humankind sometimes made war necessary, and did not shy from those fights. But he was not proud of military triumphs. "I think that 'victors' can never enjoy 'victory,'" he once wrote (*The Letters of J.R.R. Tolkien* edited by H. Carpenter with C. Tolkien, 235).

See also:
Beowulf

SPOILER— CAUTION!

WARNING:
The following chapter reveals
events towards the end of
The Lord of the Rings.

If you don't want to know how the story ends,
DO NOT READ FURTHER!

DOES
FRODO
FAIL?

HAPPILY EVER AFTER. We often want stories to end that way. Bilbo says a few times that he hopes for such an ending for himself. You probably expected it from *LOTR*, didn't you?

For all his training in ancient literature, Tolkien is a very modern writer. At the end of the story, when readers expect Frodo to act like a traditional hero, Tolkien refuses to follow an old-fashioned plot.

Instead, he finishes with a twist: Frodo fails to give up the Ring at the Crack of Doom. And it is a "failure," as Tolkien puts it—a failure of strength and will (*The Letters of J.R.R. Tolkien* edited by H. Carpenter with C. Tolkien, 325). Frodo has lost his battle against the power of the Ring. This is quite a surprise for most readers. Traditional heroes

Early *LOTR* readers had to wait a long time to learn how the story ends. Revisions, maps, and notes delayed publication of the last volume untl a year after the first two appeared.

have extraordinary strength. They do whatev-
er is necessary to overcome the forces they
face. Frodo does not.

Tolkien knew readers would have identi-
fied with Frodo up to then, and would want
to imagine that they would prove worthy on
such a difficult mission. That didn't matter to
him. He was determined that Frodo would
not end the quest with a typical heroic act.
He believed it was important to risk disap-
pointing his readers, to offer a message more
important than any emotional thrill. As
Tolkien expert

Elizabeth Scarborough puts it, "At the start of the story, Frodo is soft. He doesn't want to be special, much less a hero. He puts off leaving Hobbiton, as if the Ring problem will go away. By the end he is tougher, but is still not a storybook hero like Aragorn, who spends his life facing and conquering evil. Aragorn is hard—frighteningly so. While we admire Aragorn, we are much more like Frodo. Evil often overwhelms and confuses us. So we must rely on our trusted friends to come to our aid."

It takes the whole Fellowship—even the clownish hobbits Merry and Pippin—to defeat Sauron. Good triumphs over evil, but not because a solitary hero defeats an enemy.

THE FICKLE FINGER OF FATE?

Some people wonder if Frodo's final act is determined by fate. It's true that a lot of *LOTR* seems to be directed by a

Tolkien considered a sequel to *LOTR*, called *The New Shadow*, set a century later. After defeating evil, Gondorians would become bored with goodness. In reaction, cults would arise to worship dark powers. A palace rebellion would be planned.

But he dropped the idea. It wasn't about fighting great evil, just nasty human nature.

Just as
Tolkien picked
December 25—
Christmas—as
the beginning of
Frodo's journey,
he chose a
significant date
for the Ring's
destruction.
Sauron is
defeated on
March 25, which
once marked what
we now celebrate
as Good Friday:
the day Christ
died to overthrow
Satan.

higher power. As Gandalf tells Frodo, "Bilbo was *meant* to find the Ring, and *not* by its maker. In which case you were also *meant* to have it" (*The Lord of the Rings* by J.R.R. Tolkien, 55). Later, the members of the Fellowship come together at Rivendell even though Elrond did not summon them— another strange coincidence. At the council, Elrond seemed to know that Frodo would offer to carry the Ring. Again and again, the story seems to be driven by a guiding hand.

But Tolkien did not believe the ending is decided by fate. In his view, Ilúvatar, God of Middle-earth, does no more than throw the elements together to see what will happen— to test Frodo and the others. The choices are theirs to make. And in Frodo's case, the test is really about his ability to remain merciful to Gollum. At any moment in the story, Frodo might lose his sympathy for Gollum, as Sam does. After all, Gollum could easily kill them both.

That's one of the great messages in *LOTR*. The strength we usually see in a hero is not as important as other characteristics. Despite becoming tougher than he was at the start of the story, Frodo still has his humble hobbit virtues at the end. His softer qualities save Middle-earth. Just as Gandalf predicted,

Frodo's mercy towards Gollum makes him heroic enough to defeat Sauron. In this sense, Tolkien believed, Frodo did not fail at all. When Gollum slips on the ledge in Mount Doom, and the Ring is finally taken on the last step of the long journey, Frodo succeeds magnificently.

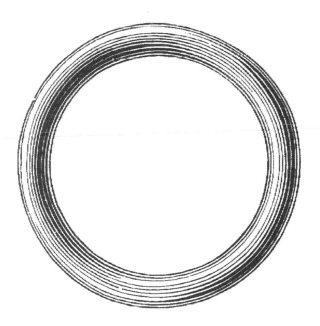

ACKNOWLEDGMENTS

I WOULD LIKE to thank the staffs of Berkley Books and Puffin Books for their support, which exceeds all expectations. At Berkley Books, along with my editor Kim Waltemyer: Leslie Gelbman, Scott Mandel, Liz Perl, Sally Franklin, and Lara Robbins. At Puffin Books, along with my editor Amanda Li: Clare Hulton, Francesca Dow, Elaine McQuade, Julie Howson, Sholto Brown, and Leah Thaxton. Many of their colleagues also supported this book directly and extensively. Thank you.

Elizabeth Scarborough, my expert Tolkien guide, read draft after draft. Without her help I would have been lost.

As ever, I am grateful to Sophie Gorell Barnes, Diana Tyler, and their colleagues at MBA Literary Agents in London; and to Michele Rubin, Maja Nikolic, and Siobhán Hayes at Writers House in New York.

Many thanks to artist Jean Pierre Targete and designer Judith Murello for a beautiful cover.

For their kindness, I would like to thank Allan Comp,

Selma Thomas, Véronique de La Bruyère, and John Warner; and for essential daily counsel, Stacy Schiff.

I would like thank Taha MacPherson and the New Zealand Embassy for their hospitality at the premiere of *The Fellowship of the Ring* in Washington, D.C.

I would also like to thank Gil Crawford for sharing what *The Lord of the Rings* means to him. It made this book mean more to me.

My parents: what can I say?

Finally, for their unfailing encouragement and friendship, I would like to thank Arif Lalani and—distinct from the rest of the world by more than just a couple of dashes—the singular Katie Kerr.

BIBLIOGRAPHY

JUST AS IN history, a lot of Tolkien scholarship can be dated "B.C."; but in this case it would mean "Before Carpenter," referring to Humphrey Carpenter, author of *Tolkien: a Biography* (1977) and editor of *The Letters of J.R.R. Tolkien* (1981). Prior to the publication of those books, some brave souls did their best—often producing very good work—with limited access to Tolkien's own thoughts about Middle-earth. Since then, nearly every worthwhile book about Tolkien, whether for a general audience or for academics, has relied on Carpenter's books as essential sources. This volume is no exception. If you are interested in knowing more about Tolkien, you are strongly urged to read at least the biography. It has the added attraction of being beautifully written. Also, it's worth noting that the value of the *Letters* book comes in large part from readers like you, who dared to write to Tolkien with questions. If a question that interests you isn't answered in this book, you may find the answer in *Letters*.

Citations from those books (as well as some others) are already alongside the quotations. As well, both titles provided valuable biographical information within this book.

In addition to them, a few books on specific subjects are notable: For a handy A-Z reference, Robert Foster's *The Complete Guide to Middle-earth*; for more about Tolkien's languages and alphabets, Ruth S. Noel's *The Languages of Tolkien's Middle-earth*; and for a lively guide to legends, Malcolm South's *Mythical and Fabulous Creatures: a Source Book and Research Guide*. Bibliographic details for these are listed below.

WORKS BY J.R.R. TOLKIEN

The Hobbit (London: G. Allen & Unwin Ltd., 1937). Houghton Mifflin trade paperback edition (2001) consulted for this work. Based on Collins Modern Classics edition (London: HarperCollins, 1998).

The Lord of the Rings (London: G. Allen & Unwin Ltd., 1954–5). Single-volume edition (HarperCollins, 1994; Boston: Mifflin Company, 1994) consulted for this work.

The Silmarillion (London: G. Allen & Unwin, 1977; Boston: Houghton Mifflin, 1977).

The Letters of J.R.R. Tolkien, selected and edited by Humphrey Carpenter, with the assistance of Christopher Tolkien (London: Allen & Unwin, 1981; Boston: Houghton Mifflin, 1981).

"Guide to the Names in *The Lord of the Rings*," reprinted in Jared Lobdell's *A Tolkien Compass*, listed below. (This work is a guide written by J.R.R. Tolkien and revised by Christopher Tolkien to help translators of *LOTR*.)

Full copyright information for Tolkien's works appears after the Notes section of this book.

WORKS ABOUT TOLKIEN

Carpenter, Humphrey. *Tolkien: a Biography* (London: G. Allen & Unwin, 1977; Boston: Houghton Mifflin, 1977).

Carpenter, Humphrey. *The Inklings: C.S. Lewis, J.R.R. Tolkien, Charles Williams and Their Friends* (London: Allen and Unwin, 1978; Boston: Houghton Mifflin, 1979).

Christensen, Bonniejean. "Character Transformation in *The Hobbit*" (article in Lobdell, see below).

Carter, Lin. *Tolkien: A Look Behind* The Lord of the Rings (New York: Ballantine, 1969).

Duriez, Colin. *Tolkien and* The Lord of the Rings: *A Guide to Middle-earth* (Mahwah, NJ: HiddenSpring/Paulist Press, 2001).

Foster, Robert. *The Complete Guide to Middle-earth*, rev. ed. (New York: Ballantine, 1979).

Grotta, Daniel. *J.R.R. Tolkien: Architect of Middle-earth: a Biography* (Philadelphia: Running Press, 1976).

Helms, Randel. *Tolkien's World* (Boston, Houghton Mifflin, 1974).

Kocher, Paul H. *Master of Middle-earth: the Fiction of J.R.R. Tolkien* (Boston: Houghton Mifflin, 1972).

Lobdell, Jared (ed.). *A Tolkien Compass: including J.R.R. Tolkien's Guide to the Names in* The Lord of The Rings (La Salle, Ill.: Open Court, 1975).

Fonstad, Karen Wynn. *The Atlas of Middle-earth*, rev. ed. (Boston: Houghton Mifflin, 1991).

Nitzsche, Jane Chance. *Tolkien's Art: a Mythology for England* (London: Macmillan, 1979).

Noel, Ruth S. *The Languages of Tolkien's Middle-earth* (Boston: Houghton Mifflin, 1980).

Noel, Ruth S. *The Mythology of Middle-earth* (Boston: Houghton Mifflin, 1977).

Shippey, T. A. *The Road to Middle-earth* (London: Allen & Unwin, 1982; Boston: Houghton Mifflin, 1983).

Stanton, Michael N. *Hobbits, Elves, and Wizards* (New York: Palgrave/St. Martin's Press, 2001).

Tyler, J. E. A. *The New Tolkien Companion*, facsimile repr. of 1976 ed. (New York: Gramercy, 2000).

GENERAL BIBLIOGRAPHY

Alexander, Michael (trans.) *Beowulf: a Verse Translation* (London: Penguin, 1973).

Bellows, Henry Adams (trans.) *The Poetic Edda*. (Princeton: Princeton University Press, 1936). Available at Internet Sacred Texts Archive (see below).

Borges, Jorge Luis, with Margarita Guerrero. *The Book of Imaginary Beings* (New York: Dutton, 1969).

Branston, Brian. *The Lost Gods of England* (New York: Oxford University Press, 1974).

Campbell, Joseph. *The Hero with a Thousand Faces* (Princeton: Princeton University Press, 1968).

Clute, John, and John Grant. *The Encyclopedia of Fantasy* (New York: St. Martin's, 1999).

Grohskopf, Bernice. *Life and Literature in Anglo-Saxon England* (New York: Atheneum, 1968).

Keightley, Thomas. *The Fairy Mythology* (London: G. Bell, 1878). (See at www.celticatlanta.com/invisibleworld/fairy_mythology)

Lang, Andrew. *The Red Fairy Book* (London: Longmans, Green, 1980).

Lönnrot, Elias. *The Kalevala*, translated by John M. Crawford, (New York: J.B. Alden, 1888). Available at Internet Sacred Texts Archive (see below).

Lönnrot, Elias. *The Kalevala*, translated by Francis Peabody Magoun Jr. (Cambridge, MA: Harvard University Press, 1963).

Nigg, Joseph. *The Book of Fabulous Beasts: a Treasury of Writings From Ancient Times to the Present* (New York: Oxford University Press, 1999).

Rose, Carol. *Giants, Monsters, and Dragons: an Encyclopedia of Folklore, Legend, and Myth* (Santa Barbara, California: ABC-CLIO, 2000).

Rose, Carol. *Spirits, Fairies, Leprechauns, and Goblins: an Encyclopedia* (New York: Norton, 1998).

South, Malcolm. *Mythical and Fabulous Creatures: a Source Book and Research Guide* (New York, Greenwood, 1987).

Sturluson, Snorri. *Prose Edda*, translated by Arthur Gilchrist Brodeur (New York: American–Scandinavian Foundation, 1916). Available at Internet Sacred Texts Archive (see below).

Wimberly, Lowry C. *Folklore in the English and Scottish Ballads* (New York: Frederick Ungar, 1959).

INTERNET RESOURCES OF SPECIAL INTEREST

Official Site (www.tolkien.co.uk)
This site, maintained by Tolkien's UK publishers, has information on various editions and interesting artwork samples, as well answers to many questions.

The Encyclopedia of Arda (www.glyphweb.com/arda)
This site offers an excellent guide to the details of Tolkien's world: who's who, where's where, what's what. A superb reference.

The Tolkien Society (www.tolkiensociety.org)
The Mythopoeic Society (www.mythsoc.org)
These two Tolkien groups are beyond mere fan clubs. If you want to talk about Tolkien with other serious readers, or to look into the literary details of Tolkien's work, these organizations will interest you.

OneRing.Net (www.theonering.net)
One Ring (onering.virbius.com.index.php)
Tolkien Online (www.tolkienonline.com)
These general sites, offering news and useful links, are good
starting points for new Tolkien fans, or for serious afficionados
who want the latest news on the films or new editions.

The Elvish Linguistic Fellowship (www.elvish.org)
Ardalambion (www.uib.no/People/hnohf)
These sites are essential for anyone interested in Tolkien's
languages. The Elvish Linguistic Fellowship is a good place to
find others who share your interest. Ardalambion is a terrific
accomplishment by Helgē Kåre Fauskanger.

Publisher's Note: Every effort has been made to ensure that the
online references in this book are appropriate and accurate.
However, information on the Internet is liable to change. We
cannot take responsibility for third-party websites. As always,
parents are strongly advised to supervise use of the Internet.

NOTES

Baggins, Frodo
"Baggings": Shippey, *Road to Middle-earth*, 56
"Caves": Though to have done so in this book would have
    revealed too much of the ending of *LOTR*, much of Frodo's
    quest can be compared to the "hero's journey" outlined by
    Joseph Campbell in *The Hero with a Thousand Faces*.
Riders of the Mark: The hillside horse is in Uffington. Some
    authorities say it dates back thousands of years.

Beowulf
"One-tenth": For facts about the history of the *Beowulf*
    manuscript, the introduction to Michael Alexander's 1973
    translation (Penguin) is useful.
"Golden Hall": Shippey, *Road to Middle-earth*, 96 (and others).
    A close comparison of the song Aragorn sings and the
    Anglo-Saxon poem "The Wanderer" shows many thematic
    connections to the "wanderer" of *LOTR*. And any reason to
    read "The Wanderer" is a good reason.

Dwarves
"Ugly, long-nosed"; "loved the light": Thomas Bulfinch's *The Age of Fable* (1913).
"The Dwarves do at times": *Teutonic Mythology* by Jacob Grimm, translated by James Steven Stallybrass (London: G. Bell, 1882)

Elves
A detailed discussion of the legends about fairies, and many ideas for further reading, can be found in Malcolm South's *Mythical and Fabulous Creatures: a Source Book and Research Guide*, cited in the bibliography of this book.
Quotation from Spenser's *The Faerie Queen*, edited by the author.

Galadriel
"The greatest spiritual power in Greece": John Warrington in *Everyman's Classical Dictionary* (London: Dent, 1961).

Gollum
"could not keep away the curse": Andrew Lang, *The Red Fairy Book*. The text of many of Andrew Lang's old fairy tale collections can be found online, for those readers interested in seeing what inspired the young Tolkien.
"new Gollum": This chapter is based on the insights found in Bonniejean Christensen's article "Character Transformation in *The Hobbit*," found in in Jared Lobdell's *A Tolkien Compass* (La Salle, Ill.: Open Court, 1975). For anyone interested in looking further into this question, Christensen's article quotes extensively from both the old and new version of *The Hobbit*. Her insights are used in this book with her permission.
"Gollum ultimately has to break your heart": quoted in *New York Post*, February 20, 2002.

Gondor
Plato's description of Atlantis from: Plato, *The Apology of Socrates; and the Crito*, translated by Benjamin Jowett (New York: Scribners, 1864). Edited by the author.

Languages
Background to the *Kalevala* from Francis Peabody Magoun Jr.'s commentary accompanying his 1963 translation, *The Kalevala*, compiled by Elias Lönnrot and translated by Francis Peabody Magoun Jr. (Cambridge, MA: Harvard University Press, 1963).

Elias Lönnrot cartoon by A. W. Linsén. From Magoun.

Quotations from the *Kalevala* taken from 1888 translation by John Martin Crawford.

"at least fourteen": Ruth S. Noel, *The Languages of Tolkien's Middle-earth* (Boston: Houghton Mifflin, 1980), 6.

Helge Kåre Fauskanger's tally from his website devoted to Tolkien linguistics, *Ardalambion* (www.uib.no/People/hnohf).

Middle-earth
"Cold arose out of Niflheim": *The Story of the Volsungs*, translated by William Morris and Eirikr Magnusson (London: Walter Scott Press, 1888).

Names
"Fródi was crowned king": Sturluson, Snorri, *The Prose Edda*, translated by Arthur Gilchrist Brodeur (New York: The American-Scandinavian Foundation, 1916). Edited by the author.

"Crack of Doom": *The Mythology of Middle-earth* by Ruth S. Noel (Boston: Houghton Mifflin, 1977). Tolkien also refers to this in his letters and his notes to translators. As mentioned earlier, the single best resource for Tolkien's names is *J.R.R. Tolkien's Guide to the Names in* The Lord of The Rings, written by Tolkien himself for his translators, and published (revised by Christopher Tolkien) in Jared Lobdell's *A Tolkien Compass* (La Salle, Ill.: Open Court, 1975). However, for those now interested in this subject, the best insights have reappeared in sources that are more readily available.

Orcs

Orc (sea monster): Thomas Bulfinch, *Age of Fable: Legends of Charlemagne*, 1913.
The Princess and the Goblin by George Macdonald (London: Strahan, 1872).

Riddles

"I saw four fine creatures" adapted from: *The Exeter Riddle Book* by Kevin Crossley-Holland (London: Penguin, 1993). Interesting background to ancient riddles can be found in the same source.

Sauron

"point by point": Randel Helms, *Tolkien's World* (Boston: Houghton Mifflin, 1974), 68.

Spiders

"in which there was much sin": Lord Dunsany (Edward John Moreton Drax Plunkett), *The Fortress Unvanquishable Save for Sacnoth* (London: George Allen, 1908).

Swords

"King Volsung built" and "clad in a blue cloak": *The Story of the Volsungs*, translated by William Morris and Eirikr Magnusson (London: Walter Scott Press, 1888).

Towers
The classic work about towers is a poem by Robert Burns, "Childe Roland to the Dark Tower Came" (1855). However, as John Clute and John Grant point out in their excellent reference *The Encyclopedia of Fantasy*, the genre remains fresh, with modern skyscrapers standing in for medieval towers, as in Diane Duane's *So You Want to Be a Wizard?*

Spoiler
Elizabeth Scarborough quoted from personal correspondence.

All illustrations from the Dover Clip Art Collection or www.ArtToday.com, except for page 76 (see *Notes*: Languages).

INDEX

ABOUT THE AUTHOR

David Colbert is the author of *The Magical Worlds of Harry Potter: a Treasury of Myths, Legends and Fascinating Facts,* also available from Berkley Books, as well as the *Eyewitness* history series. A graduate of Brown University, he studied anthropology and mythology but spent most of his time reading randomly in the library, which is pretty much what he still does.